For 75 years, God has
of IFES, enabling peo[
appropriate that, in cel
produced an excellent de
ministry of IFES, this d
ongoing work. IFES insid
by insights from Scriptur
from global IFES staff.

WALTER KIM
PRESIDENT OF THE NATIONAL ASSOCIATION OF EVANGELICALS

The deepest, truest learning is always over the shoulder and
through the heart. In *The Unfinished Story* we are graced to learn
from a wise, practised teacher of Scripture with a lifelong love
for students. Through a month of reflections that weave together
biblical text with prayers and psalms, David J Montgomery
draws us into the story of those whose encounter with Jesus was
'a taster of the kingdom to come', inviting us into a way of reading
the Bible that is, at one and the same time, 'for me, to me, about
me, from me, and within me' – which is as it should be, as we
engage Luke's story, a story which is the heart of the gospel that
continues to be written in every century and every culture.

STEVEN GARBER
*SENIOR FELLOW FOR VOCATION AND THE COMMON GOOD, MJ
MURDOCK CHARITABLE TRUST, AND AUTHOR OF* VISIONS OF
VOCATION: COMMON GRACE FOR THE COMMON GOOD

It was with great joy that I read the book that my colleague and
friend Monty has prepared. His way of writing and presenting
these devotionals is very special. First, because they follow the
good tradition of Scripture Engagement in IFES, where the main
point is to invite us to a personal encounter with the Lord through
the Scriptures. Going through Luke and Acts, reflecting on these
selected passages, connecting with the reality of the student work
through the beautiful stories shared and with his touch of personal
perspective here and there, all create a very welcoming environment
for this encounter with the Lord in the Word. Also, the invitations to

wider readings that give us context to the great and wonderful story, the prayers that help us respond and the connections to the Psalms to be used at the end of the day help us to interact with the Word in different and inspiring ways. An excellent contribution from Monty so that we continue to celebrate many IFES anniversaries loving, studying, living and sharing the Scriptures.

RICARDO BORGES
IFES SECRETARY FOR SCRIPTURE ENGAGEMENT

This book by Dr David J Montgomery provides a helpful way to explore Luke's two contributions to the New Testament (Luke's Gospel and the Acts of the Apostles). The way in which the passage of Scripture is opened up for us each day provides a model of solid Biblical study, done with a devotional heart. The stories which are mingled into the exposition, many of them from people touched by the ministry of IFES, bring personal application of the themes being discussed and underline the book's other purpose, namely, to mark the 75th anniversary of IFES. It is also delightful to see a Psalm for each evening, in a day when the Psalms have become somewhat neglected in the worshipping life of the church. I thoroughly commend this book.

THE REV PROFESSOR ATB MCGOWAN
DIRECTOR OF THE RUTHERFORD CENTRE FOR REFORMED
THEOLOGY

Luke's Gospel – and his sequel, Acts – record how God's redemption story found its climax in the death and resurrection of Jesus, and as the Good News was preached to all nations, starting in Jerusalem. This story hasn't finished, and students in IFES movements across the globe are living and speaking for Jesus in remarkable ways. As Monty invites us to meet Jesus afresh, and introduces us to students around the world following him, expect to have your own heart changed and your passion for student ministry stirred.

PETER DRAY
INTERIM EXECUTIVE DIRECTOR, UCCF; CO-AUTHOR OF REALITY
AND OTHER STORIES

THE UNFINISHED STORY

To our god-daughters, Paige and Hanna

Be students of the Word

THE UNFINISHED STORY

THIRTY DAYS IN LUKE AND ACTS

DAVID J MONTGOMERY

Foreword by Tim Adams, General Secretary of IFES

Muddy
Pearl

Published in 2023 by

Muddy Pearl, Edinburgh, Scotland.

www.muddypearl.com

books@muddypearl.com

British Library Cataloguing in Publication Data.

A catalogue record for this book is available from the British Library

ISBN 978-1-914553-16-5

Typeset in Minion by Revo Creative Ltd, Lancaster

Printed in Great Britain by Bell & Bain Ltd, Glasgow

FOREWORD

When you read the history of student ministry and the early beginnings of IFES it reads a bit like the book of Acts. There are perilous voyages, stories of God's miraculous provision and student movements emerging in many different countries at the same time.

For example, IFES' first connection in the Caribbean came when the plane that Stacey Woods (the first IFES General Secretary) was travelling on had engine problems and was forced to land in Jamaica for a few days to be repaired. During that short time in Jamaica, Stacey connected with local church leaders and learned that the University of the West Indies was opening its first campus there later that year. The Christian student movement in Jamaica was soon formed and the partnership with IFES continues to this day.

A few weeks ago, I was in Nigeria and met Kola Ejiwunmi (known as Uncle Kola), the first staff worker of the IFES movement in Nigeria, NIFES. The stories he told of his epic journeys, travelling on foot and by bus all around Nigeria in the 1960s and 70s, certainly had the feel of an apostolic adventure.

So, what better way to recognise our 75th anniversary than to look back to that even more significant story of beginnings, the story of the first apostles and the emergence of the church as described in the book of Acts. In my first months as General Secretary, this was the book I reflected on in my personal devotion time, and I am thankful to David Montgomery for bringing me back to it again. In Acts, we are reminded of the fragility and vulnerability of our human nature, the transforming power of the Holy Spirit, and God's amazing grace and mercy. We see clearly that God alone is the ultimate author, not just of the story of Acts, but the story of the church, of IFES and of our lives.

The theme of our 75th anniversary is *Unfinished: Living God's story in the university.* As well as using this milestone as an opportunity to look back and give thanks to God for all he has done since IFES was founded, we also take this moment to recognize that we have much more to look forward to and pray for. The global student population has more than doubled since the year 2000 and continues to grow. Students today face a plethora of stresses and uncertainty, and they need the hope of the gospel as much as ever. In this context, our vision is to see students thriving together as communities of disciples and impacting the university, the church, and society for the glory of Christ. This story, God's story in the university, remains unfinished, and we are committed to playing our part.

The book of Acts connects with this theme of an unfinished story. In itself Acts is a continuation of the Gospel of Luke, which is 'an orderly account' (Luke 1:3) of 'all that Jesus began to do and teach' (Acts 1:1). You cannot read Luke without reading Acts, and you cannot read Acts without being left wondering what happens next and it is itself a healthy reminder that God's story continues. There is a thread that runs from the Gospel of Luke through the book of Acts to the early beginnings of IFES, and it continues into your life as you navigate this month of devotions. By God's grace, we are invited to be a part of this great story, and I pray that this month of devotions will encourage and inspire you as you play your God-given role.

TIM ADAMS
IFES GENERAL SECRETARY

Oxford, UK
March 2023

PREFACE

The Bible is a lamp to our feet and a light for our path. It is healing for the soul; it is the breath of God himself. Through it, God challenges and comforts, rebukes and restores, exhorts and encourages. It is, in its entirety, God's revelation of himself to us.

The Bible can also be misused. Not just in obvious ways by the abusive and unscrupulous, but also by well-meaning Christians who, often in an effort to make it 'personally relevant', take verses of Scripture and make them mean things they were never intended to mean. That is why Bible study is important: it is learning to understand Scripture in its own terms, respecting the context and obeying the message, no matter how uncomfortable it makes us feel.

However, Bible study can easily become an abstract thing; too much brain activity and not enough heart-engagement. I am privileged to work for the International Fellowship of Evangelical Students (IFES) and I love how one of our core values is not simply 'The Bible', but 'Scripture engagement'. All Bible study should primarily and ultimately not be about us, but about God, his relationship with us, and how we can experience him.

I remember Darrell Johnson being interviewed at the 2015 World Assembly and sharing how, before he opened a passage to prepare for preaching, he asked himself (referencing the Song of Solomon): 'What does this passage tell me about him whom my heart loves?' That should be the question for all of us when we open Scripture at any time, regardless of our background or previous experience with the Bible.

Speaking personally, my journey with Scripture

has gone through various stages. I was privileged to be taught it as an infant sitting at my parents' feet, and was fascinated by it as a listener: it was a bedtime story *for me*. In adolescence, as I committed my life to Christ and read it regularly as a spiritual discipline, I saw it as a story *to me*; a set of exhortations to help me live well as a disciple.

Then, as I grew in the faith, I realized it was a story *about me*; I saw more clearly my own shortcomings in the lives of its flawed heroes and marvelled at the sufficiency of Christ to cover all my sin. As I studied it more deeply in seminary and embarked on a preaching ministry, it became (not always for the best) a story *from me*; truths that I felt commissioned to pass on to others. Eventually I realized that these strands all needed to come together and, as I grasped more firmly the depth of God's grace, they became a story growing *within me*.

As we engage with Scripture, the Spirit who inspired those authors is the same Spirit who is convicting and, hopefully, changing us.

This book is written to commemorate God's faithfulness to IFES over seventy-five years. However, it is also written for all who are interested in going deeper in their own engagement with Scripture, and to hear something of the way God has been at work among students and graduates over the decades. Since 1947 generations of students have sought to fulfill the vision of the founders of IFES: to plant an evangelical Christian witness in every university in the world. It is a missionary vision founded on the missionary heart of God.

This devotional aims to take us through two important books in the New Testament which outline the story of Jesus and the church he planted. They are both written by Luke who was an eyewitness of the birth and growth of the Christian church.

As a historian, his work has been carefully researched (Luke 1:3; Acts 1:1–3); as a medic, he has a particular interest in verifying and reporting the many healings carried out by Jesus and his disciples; as a Gentile, he has an eye for the outsider, the poor and those who often felt excluded by traditional religion. He shows how Jesus opened the kingdom of God to those on the margins, both inside and outside Israel. Similarly, he reports on how the Old Testament's vision of God blessing all nations began to be realized more fully in Paul's missionary journeys throughout the Graeco-Roman world.

How to use this book

The devotionals aim to dig a little deeper into the passage so that the reader will not only find some inspirational thought for the day, but will also understand the text and grasp some of the main themes that Luke uses to frame his story of Jesus and the church. To get the most out of this book you should plan to set aside enough time to:

Pray: Before you do anything else, ask the Lord to open your heart and mind to his Word, and to give you understanding.

Read: Then, open your Bible and read the original text. Some of the passages are quite long, but it is important to read them all in order to understand both their context and message.

Reflect: After reading the comments in the devotional, take time to consider your own reflections on the passage – meditating on it and perhaps journaling the things God has specifically been saying to *you* through his Word.

Respond: Use the prayer as a means of beginning your own time of prayer and response to the day's readings, and ask for wisdom in how to apply them. The prayers for the Acts passages have been written by IFES colleagues around the world.

I hope that this book may also inspire you and give you the confidence to study the whole of Luke and Acts yourself. That is why I have included 'The Wider Story' section featuring questions and comments to help you understand what is happening in the passages not covered by the devotional. In this way you'll be able to appreciate each day's passage in its wider context.

We conclude each section with 'An Evening Psalm', chosen for its connection with the day's theme.

For those who are time-poor but don't want to rush the experience, an alternative approach could be to spend a week reflecting on each 'Day' of the devotional – especially if you want to tackle the 'The Wider Story' section as well. This approach could also have the advantage of giving you seven days to reflect on the Evening Psalm before you sleep.

However you choose to use it, my prayer is that by the end of this book you will not only know more about the mission of God, but you will know him and be inspired to serve him faithfully and with full assurance of the inheritance he has promised us all: 'rejoice that your names are written in heaven' (Luke 10:20).

DAVID J MONTGOMERY
WHITEROCK, CO. DOWN, ST. PATRICK'S DAY 2023

ACKNOWLEDGEMENTS

I would like to thank Tim Adams and John Bagg of IFES for encouraging me to write this for its seventy-fifth anniversary; to Jill Bain and others at the IFES Oxford office, who helped me access stories and all who helped make this a reality in time for the 2023 World Assembly. Thanks to Luke Cawley for stepping in with advice when an earlier project had stalled. Thanks also to those who read and commented so kindly on the manuscript; to translators Dorcas Gonzalez and Stephanie Tharp; to proofreaders Anja Rajaobelina-Morvan and Pierre-André Joset; and to Eliza Justice who has coordinated this important work. I want to record my special appreciation to all those at Muddy Pearl, especially my editor Stephanie Heald for her hard work and encouragement.

Personally, I want to acknowledge: David and Laura Jennings whose homes have been places of retreat where many of these pages were first written; my colleagues on the IFES Europe team, including my PA, Lorna Moore, who sometimes had to wait longer than they should have for answers to emails while I finished this book; and my other global colleagues who supplied the prayers for Acts.

Above all, thanks to my wife Gwen who, as well as writing many of the prayers for the Luke section, has been a constant gift and support to me in life and ministry.

CONTENTS

PART 2: ACTS

PART 1: LUKE

THE PROMISE

READ: LUKE 1:1–4, 26–56

> *You will conceive and give birth to a son, and you are to call him Jesus.*
>
> LUKE 1:31

The story of Jesus is the central pivot on which everything else hinges. His life and ministry look back at all that God had done in the Old Testament, and look forward to what he will continue to achieve through his new covenant people, the church.

Luke is different from the other Gospel writers in that he was a non-Jew and, in his Gospel, he has a particular interest in Jesus' embrace of the outsiders: the Gentiles, the poor, the outcasts and those who often felt excluded by traditional religion. He was a historian and his two volumes were carefully researched (Luke 1:3; Acts 1:1–3); he was also a physician, so you may notice many of the healing miracles reported with a doctor's eye. At the end of the Gospel (Luke 24:27, 45) we read of Jesus opening the Scriptures to his disciples and showing how from the beginning all Scripture testified about him. So let us meet him as he is introduced to us by Luke.

There is clearly something special happening here. Luke writes of a supernatural visitor announcing a supernatural birth. If God was about to do something unprecedented, and if this child, Jesus, was indeed to be different, then we should not be surprised that the circumstances of his birth are also unique.

God in history

Look for the historical markers: Luke says he has researched thoroughly (verse 3) and that he has sourced eyewitness accounts (verse 2). Notice the references to places, times and dates (verses 5, 26, 39, 56). These are special days marked by God's supernatural intervention, but Luke is also careful to establish the historical reality of what was happening.

God through history

Luke also tells us that these events have a context. While they are unexpected for the main actors in the story (Mary, Joseph, Zechariah), they are in line with what God has been planning all along. Look for how this story mentions previous stories – those of David, Jacob, Abraham (verses 27, 32, 33, 55) – and how the characters see themselves as part of the bigger story of God's unfolding purposes through generations past and future (verses 48, 50). God had promised this day would come, and 'no word from God will ever fail' (verse 37).

God beyond history

Although the story is firmly rooted in space and time, the real action is taking place elsewhere. God is the one who establishes governments and changes regimes and who will bring justice (verses 51–53), and he sends his messenger to announce the birth of a child supernaturally conceived who would be none other than the Son of God (verses 26, 35). This is indeed the focal point of history: God breaking into his creation, to save it (see Luke 1:76–79).

As heaven and earth meet in this story, and as Mary encounters the divine, notice her changing emotions from fear (verse 29) to questioning (verse 34) to humble obedience (verse 38), and finally to inexpressible joy (verses 46–47). Think on how these emotions can mark our own encounters with God. Mary would still have many questions – and fears – ahead of her, but her willingness to be open to the will of God and her final posture of praise and deep joy should inspire any of us who want to be 'the Lord's servant' (verse 38).

A student story

I think of Kristine who found herself in a strange country. She was from a small island and had gone to East Asia to study for her master's. She was desperately alone and was called 'outsider' by many of the other students, but she was determined to be available to witness to Jesus in any way possible. She just didn't know how. Soon however, being an 'outsider' opened doors for her to teach English to her neighbours. Then she connected with the small IFES group in the university, and little by little, as she and the other students studied the Scriptures regularly, they were encouraged through listening to God's Word to be more committed in sharing their faith. They did this, knowing that, in their country, evangelism is about investing in people in the long term until they understand and can see the truth of the gospel. Kristine's willingness to battle through her loneliness and be available to Jesus, to obey his Word and trust his promises, echoes that of Mary in this passage.

PRAY:

> Lord God, I praise you for your faithfulness throughout history. Thank you that you did not abandon your creation but intervened to save us. Like Mary, I have many questions and fears, but, like her, I want to be your humble and obedient servant, and I want to experience the deep joy that prompted her song of praise. This year give me glimpses of your glory that my soul may glorify you and my spirit rejoice in you, God, my Saviour. Amen.

THE WIDER STORY

READ: LUKE 1:5–25, 57–80

The rest of Luke 1 tells the parallel story of the birth of Jesus' cousin, John. Verses 5–25 tell of a similar supernatural announcement; then verses 57–80 recount the birth of John and his father's song of praise (paralleling Mary's song). Look for the similarities in the songs, especially God's faithfulness to his people through the generations and his care for the humble and those in need.

REFLECT:

- What does the song of Zechariah teach us about God's character and purposes?
- How does it encourage or challenge you?

AN EVENING PSALM

READ: PSALM 75

This psalm proclaims God as judge and king. The 'horn' (verses 4, 5, 10) is a symbol of kingly strength: Zechariah mentions it in his song about the new king to be born (Luke 1:69). Similarly, verse 7: 'It is God who judges: he brings one down, he exalts another' may have been in Mary's mind when she sang her song (Luke 1:52). Like the songs in Luke 1, it is a psalm about God's judgment on the arrogant, his dethroning of the powerful and wicked, and his raising up of the humble and righteous. So how will we respond to such an awesome God of justice?

The phrase 'as for me' (verse 9) is a popular one in this section of the Psalms (see 69:29; 70:5; 71:14; 73:2); it draws a contrast between how the world *seems* and how it *is*; or between how *others* are responding and how *we* should respond. 'As for me' are three simple words of faith (just one word in the Hebrew!). The psalmist does not know exactly how things will work out, but he is resolved to be faithful to God. In this psalm he is resolved to 'declare' what God has done (verse 9) – also translated as 'proclaim', a mission word (verse 9, NLT). Even though evil seems to be all around, God's justice will come. Reflect on the things that may cause you to doubt or stumble in your walk with God, and in faith, like Mary and Zechariah, pray the words of verses 9–10.

DAY 2

GOOD NEWS FOR EVERYONE

READ: LUKE 2:1–21

> *But the angel said to them, 'Do not be afraid. I bring you good news that will cause great joy for all the people.'*

LUKE 2:10

If this is indeed the centre of history, the moment when God intervenes intimately and personally in his creation, perhaps we would expect a fireworks display. Surely an event of such global significance demanded nothing less. However, reading this story we are likely to be a little underwhelmed by its sheer 'ordinariness'. The circumstances of the birth are so humble they are outrageous, even insulting! The Son of God was born in a crowded house and laid in a feeding trough.

Yet the story is an amazing combination of the ordinary and the extraordinary, the natural and the supernatural. Luke continues with his historical markers (verses 1–4) while we also get the first hint of the place of the poor and the outsider in God's purposes.

Ordinary people

There is nothing special about Mary and Joseph other than their willingness to be obedient to God (Luke 1:38; Matthew 1:24), and there is certainly nothing special about the first witnesses. While King Herod sat in his palace with his personal theologians who were too lazy or spiritually blind to follow the clues and check out the facts (Matthew 2:3–8), and while the best brains in the Orient took months of searching before reaching their destination (Matthew 2:1–12), a few farmhands on the hills outside Bethlehem were given a special visitation from God, listened to the instructions and found the baby immediately. These casual labourers on the night watch – the shift nobody wanted – were the first to hear something that would shake the world.

Extraordinary news

Another contrast in this story is between the terror caused by the messengers and the amazing joy of the message itself. Nobody, not even strong, hardened hill-farmers, can encounter an army of angels and remain cool; but as they thought about the actual content of what was said, terror was replaced with wonder and excitement. They were given an invitation to go and join the party! Invitations to a royal baby shower were not usually part of a Bethlehem shepherd's social calendar.

Perhaps you are familiar with one of those 'word map' tools, where you feed in a document to software and it gives you a pictorial representation of the most common or important words. Well, think of how a word map of Luke 2:10–11 would look: the words in the largest print would be *'no fear'*, *'news'*, *'joy'*, *'salvation'* and *'Messiah'*. Already we can see how the main characters are being changed by the arrival of Jesus. For the shepherds it was a case of 'Come, see; go, tell'. They wasted no time in leaving their posts and running to see what was going on. They accepted the invitation and then spread the word to anyone who would listen. Encountering Jesus can have that effect on you!

Then 'Mary treasured up all these' events and reflected on them in the days to come (verse 19). As she spent years in the ordinary, mundane tasks of being a mother, she was bound to have had days when she wondered if all these promises about her firstborn were true or imaginary. It must have been during these times that she would recall the arrival of the unexpected visitors from the hills with their story of an angel's visit and a heavenly chorus, and continued to believe.

How might we be helped by reflecting on this story today? The shepherds were told that the Saviour was born for *them* (verse 11), and that the message was 'for *all* … people' (verse 10, my emphasis), for 'those in whom God delights' (the literal meaning of verse 14). This event was for *us*! The invitation to the shepherds is extended to us; the 'good news' that filled them with joy can do the same to us.

PRAY:

Lord Jesus, thank you that from the beginning you demonstrated that neither wealth, nor social status, nor education, nor human achievement mattered in terms of who was invited to share in the Good News. You were born in poverty and raised in obscurity, and throughout your ministry you blessed those who had little and imagined themselves to be beyond your grace. Give me your humility and your heart. Help me to respond to your invitation with the spontaneous joy of the shepherds and, as I follow you, to reflect like Mary on your amazing kindness to your people. Amen.

THE WIDER STORY

READ: LUKE 2:22 – 4:13

The Gospels are not traditional biographies, so we know hardly anything about Jesus' childhood or young adulthood. The little we do know can be found in Luke's Gospel, Chapter 2. Firstly, there are the two temple stories (2:22–40): his parents bring him there as an infant where his special role is affirmed by two old believers (and another 'song'!). Then his parents bring him there again as a 12-year-old when we have a premonition of his later teaching ministry as all the scholars are amazed at his understanding of the Scriptures (Luke 2:41–52), what Jesus referred to as his 'Father's business' (verse 49, NKJV). Chapter 3 introduces us to the ministry of John the Baptist, and Jesus' own baptism, followed by his temptation by Satan in 4:1–13. Luke's genealogy of Jesus outlined in Chapter 3:23–28 differs from Matthew 1 in that it is traced through a different grandparent and goes right back to Adam, emphasizing the humanity of Jesus.

REFLECT:

- What can you see from the stories of Jesus' childhood (including the genealogy) that reveal more of his identity and mission?
- Do you notice anything surprising in Luke 3:1–2?
- How would you summarize John's sermons and what do they teach us about repentance?
- What can we learn from how Jesus responds to Satan's temptations?

AN EVENING PSALM

READ: PSALM 85

Psalm 85 is a prayer for revival. Can God do something to turn his people's hearts towards him again? The Christmas event inaugurated the answer to that prayer. Verse 7: 'show us your unfailing love ... and grant us your salvation', and the promise of peace in verse 8 are echoed in the song of Zechariah and also of Simeon in Luke 2:29–30. Verse 10 is a poetic summary of what the kingdom of God looks like. It pictures love (translated as 'mercy' in the NKJV version), faithfulness (translated as 'truth' in the NLT version), righteousness and peace, meeting and embracing.

All of these virtues merge in the one unique person of Jesus Christ. He not only embodies the love of God, he also said 'I am ... the truth' (John 14:6); he was the one whom prophets called the 'sun of righteousness' (Malachi 4:2), and the 'Prince of Peace' (Isaiah 9:6). Psalm 85:10 became incarnate at Bethlehem! Re-read verses 4–7 and use them as a prayer that God would revive your heart this week.

REJECTED AT HOME

READ: LUKE 4:14–30

> *The Spirit of the Lord is on me, because he has anointed me to proclaim good news … the year of the Lord's favour.*
> LUKE 4:18–19

Playing at home may give you an edge on the sports field, but Jesus says it is often a disadvantage for a prophet (verse 24). And that applies to anyone who wants to speak God's words or live a life of discipleship today. Home is the toughest gig; the hardest setting. This is the moment that Jesus emerges onto the scene and begins his public ministry. It is his declaration of intent, his manifesto, and it sets the scene for the following three years. The passage contains themes which will recur throughout the four Gospels: Jesus teaching from Scripture, his claim of divine authority, his challenging the unbelief of his own people, and their rejection of him. We see also how news spread quickly (probably regarding his miracles – verses 14, 23) and how popular he was with many (verses 15, 22) but how some were so angry that they sought to kill him (verses 28–29). Yet God protected him (verse 30) until the moment was right for him to die. We will see all of these themes repeated time and again.

Jesus read from the Old Testament prophet Isaiah. It is actually a weaving together of two passages, to make the point that his hearers have a choice to make. How will they respond to him during this window of opportunity, this 'year of the Lord's favour' (verse 19)?

Good news for many people

Quoting from Isaiah 61:1–2 and 58:6, Jesus singles out a number of people he has come to help: the poor, the blind, the prisoners, the downtrodden and oppressed (Isaiah also mentions the brokenhearted). Jesus is preparing his listeners for the fact that his grace and salvation will be accepted most readily by those who have nothing to lose. The freedom and healing he offers will be gladly received by those who know that they are lacking – spiritually and materially.

As we read Luke's Gospel, notice how true this is. There are multiple healings of the blind and the poor. He may not have released any prisoners during his ministry (although a number of miraculous prison breaks do feature in Luke's second volume – see Acts 12; 16) but there is no doubt that Jesus' ministry brought great freedom, especially to those possessed by evil spirits or trapped in a cycle of sin.

Difficult news for some people

However, it wasn't good news for everyone. Jesus knew what they were thinking (verse 23) and reminded them that, even in their own history, God often passed over the unbelievers and sceptics within his people and graciously healed and saved those foreigners, and even enemies, whom the Israelites would have despised (verses 25–27). It didn't matter what race they were, nor whether they were materially poor like the starving widow (verse 26) or rich and of high status like the army commander Naaman (verse 27); God's grace was for all who trusted him. This news would have been difficult to swallow for many of the self-righteous religious people at church in the synagogue that day – as it still is for many.

Important news for all people

However, although he really annoyed his home congregation by speaking of God's love for their ethnic and political enemies in Sidon and Syria, the most controversial thing Jesus said that day was his claim that he, the carpenter's son, was the promised Messiah prophesied by Isaiah (verses 21–22). That is why their (and our) response to Jesus is so crucial. As he quotes Isaiah 61:2, he stops halfway through the verse and doesn't complete it. The full verse from Isaiah actually says: 'the year of the LORD's favour, and the day of vengeance of our God.' But Jesus is making the point that *now* is that day of God's favour, the time when we can see the grace of God revealed in the ministry of his Messiah, Jesus, and respond humbly to his call to follow him. The rest of Isaiah 61:2, 'the day of vengeance', will be fulfilled on a later day when he will judge the world (see Acts 17:31), but this is a day of important news. While some will resent the message and kill the messenger, for those who know their need of healing and who yearn for freedom, the day of salvation has arrived!

PRAY:

Lord Jesus, give me hope because I am spiritually poor and have nothing to give you; release me for I feel like I am in chains; heal my heart, for it is broken; help me see for I am blind; raise me up for I am downtrodden. Lord, today I respond anew to your grace; by your Spirit may I have the courage to announce 'the day of your favour' to all who will have ears to listen. In your precious name I pray, Amen.

THE WIDER STORY

READ: LUKE 4:31 – 6:49

Having proclaimed release to the prisoners, Jesus immediately sets free those imprisoned by demonic possession and other diseases (4:31–41). But he does not see these healings as the main purpose of his ministry; they are simply accompanying signs to his main calling to preach that the kingdom of God has arrived (4:42–44). In Chapter 5 another miracle accompanies his assembling of his team of disciples (5:1–11, 27–32; 6:12–16), but notice how many of his miracles bring him into conflict with the religious Pharisees – a conflict which would be present throughout his whole ministry (5:12–26, 33–39; 6:1–11). The rest of Chapter 6 is a summary of many of the key aspects of Jesus' teaching about the kingdom, a 'sermon' which Matthew records in much greater detail (Matthew 5 – 7).

REFLECT:

Signs, friends and enemies!

- Signs: What do the signs (miracles) of Luke 6:17–19, and the sermon of Luke 6:20–49, teach us about the heart of Jesus and the nature of his kingdom?
- Friends: what do we learn when we consider the type of people he chose to be his friends?
- Enemies: what was it about his ministry that his enemies disliked so much?

In light of this, what can we learn about the qualifications for discipleship and what following Jesus might involve for us?

AN EVENING PSALM

READ: PSALM 69:1–18

This is one of many psalms written at a time of despair and hopelessness, crying out for God's help (verses 1–3). The first eighteen verses tell of a string of injustices that the songwriter has experienced. Jesus would have felt many of these keenly, not least the pain of being misunderstood in his home town and by members of his own family (verse 8). It is a prayer for all who have felt the pain of similar misunderstandings and who have been mocked for no reason (verses 10–12). Jesus, in his humanity, may have cried out these words (which he would have known well) on many occasions. But, in his divinity, the resurrected Jesus is also the answer to our very same cries of despair. If you are feeling mocked and misunderstood this evening, pray verses 16–18 that you might know the boundless love and mercy of God and experience his deliverance.

SURPRISING FAITH

READ: LUKE 7:1–17

> *Then [Jesus] went up and touched the bier they were carrying … He said, 'Young man, I say to you, get up!' The dead man sat up and began to talk, and Jesus gave him back to his mother.*
>
> LUKE 7:14–15

These two healings are quite different. In one, Jesus is not even present; in the other, he gets up close and personal. In one, he is approached for a favour by a man of wealth and status; in the other, without being asked, he helps a poor, bereaved widow whose only means of financial support has gone. However, there are also a number of interesting similarities.

The reality of death

Both of the families are faced with the reality of death: one young man is on the brink of death, the other is actually in the coffin. In both cases all hope of human help has been exhausted. Jesus is approached by the centurion's friends as a last resort, while the community in Nain have given up completely. Here, Jesus shows that no circumstances are so extreme that they cannot be redeemed by him.

The authority of Jesus

The Gentile centurion displays incredible insight; according to Jesus, more than could be found among even the most religious of Jews (verse 9). He discerned the holiness of Jesus to the extent that he, a person of status within the army of occupation, did not feel worthy to let this landless, homeless, itinerant rabbi from the occupied nation come into his home! He also knew that he was only able to give commands because he in turn was under the authority of his commanding officer. The centurion's words, 'I myself' (verse 8), could mean 'I, *like you*'. He recognized that Jesus' power came from somewhere higher, so he asks Jesus to simply speak the command, and his servant would be healed (verse 7). This man recognized both the holiness and the divine power of Jesus.

In the second story, Jesus demonstrates that power by bringing a corpse back to life. If it was a movie we would see two contrasting processions moving towards each other. First, the procession of death leaving the village with pipers and mourners wailing and weeping, preceded by death itself in the form of the coffin. And second, a procession of *life* as Jesus the life-giver leads his entourage into the village, until the two processions meet and life wins! As Luke continues to reveal the identity of Jesus, we, the readers, are left to reflect on the amazing fact that this man is against death and *for* life.

Grace for the outsider

The centurion was unusual in that he seems to have been well-loved by the Jewish people and had been generous towards them. But he was still a Gentile and an enemy soldier. In addition, the sick man who needed Jesus' help was a slave. The woman of Nain may have been a Jew, but without the structure of family around her she would have been helpless and destitute. With her husband and only son gone, her future was bleak at a time when she should have been able to look forward to finishing her days without care or anxiety. In these stories Jesus' grace is poured out on: a Roman (who was an enemy soldier), a slave, a woman (who was a widow) and a dead man! Few sections in the Bible illustrate so concisely that God's grace is for all, particularly those whom we could so easily despise or overlook. This should not surprise us since Jesus here reflects the character of his Father who is a father to the fatherless and a defender of widows (Psalm 68:5), and it is this that James later tells us is the mark of true religion: 'Religion that God our Father accepts as pure and faultless is this: to look after orphans and widows in their distress' (James 1:27).

A student story

Greg, the leader of a Greek student group, has felt a particular calling to work with the growing number of alienated and disaffected students and young people in the colleges and cities in the north of the country. Many of these young people have gathered together in quasi-anarchist groups – but have shown themselves to have a greater social conscience than many Christians and have started to help migrants and the homeless. Because he had been in groups like this before his conversion, Greg found it easy to identify with their disillusionment and, seeing their compassion for others, he encouraged his group to join with these others students in their projects. The quasi-anarchist group eventually asked Greg if he would be their leader 'even though,' they joked, 'you are not a real anarchist!' Since then he has had constant opportunities to share his faith and open the Scriptures with these people and has witnessed their spiritual openness. He has seen many cultural barriers broken down and has broken many of their presuppositions about Christianity.

The vulnerability of Jesus

One final feature of today's story is how Jesus is prepared to make himself vulnerable and 'unclean' because of his compassion for others. We have seen how he did not need to be present in order to heal. Here, he could have shouted at a distance and the dead man would have been raised. But he chooses to get close to the grieving widow, personally handing her son back to her, like it was the best present she could ever receive. In the same way that he chose to get even closer to the coffin, touching it and risking being regarded as 'unclean' according to the laws of his religion (see Numbers 19:11, 16). Jesus shows how far he is prepared to go to bring life and hope to his people. As his crucifixion would demonstrate even more powerfully, death would be defeated finally and decisively, not at a distance, but intimately and personally, as he himself became subject to death in order to destroy its power and sting.

PRAY:

Lord God, I praise you that your love and grace are measureless, your compassion is limitless, your power is boundless. I praise you that you died so that I could live, you became unclean so I could be clean. I thank you that not even death need hold any fear for me. At times when it feels like I am living in the midst of a procession of death, help me to fix my eyes on your triumphant procession of life, and strengthen me to truly live until you call me home. Amen.

THE WIDER STORY

READ LUKE 7:36 – 8:21

We will look at the next section of Chapter 7 tomorrow, and then skip ahead to Chapter 9. In between these sections, we have a couple of stories that illustrate how Jesus redefined what it meant to be part of his family. In Luke 7:36–50, Jesus is honoured and anointed by a sinful woman (probably a prostitute) while being hosted by Simon, a Pharisee. Jesus accepts and blesses the woman and rebukes his host. Notice also how prominently women feature in his ministry – unheard of for a prominent Rabbi (8:1–3). Here Jesus was embracing the outcasts and causing discomfort among those who thought of themselves as God's people. He emphasizes this in Luke 8:16–21 after telling the story of the sower and the soils (8:4–15) in which he explains why there are so many different responses to hearing God's Word: disbelief, initial enthusiasm without rootedness, acceptance without wholehearted commitment, and fruitfulness.

REFLECT:

- Consider the ways in which we might be like Simon, the Pharisee. How can Jesus' rebuke in Luke 7:44–47 help us in our own discipleship?
- How can the parable of the sower help us face disappointment when others reject our message, or 'fall away' (8:13)?
- How might Luke 8:19–21 encourage those whose family members don't understand, or are even hostile to, their love for Christ?

AN EVENING PSALM

READ: PSALM 6

This prayer for deliverance reminds us of the anguish we may go through from time to time, crying out for God to help us in trouble or save us from some disaster (verse 3). Like the centurion or the bereaved and grieving mother in this morning's reading, the psalmist faces the reality of death (verses 4–5) and there have been days and nights of tears (verses 6–7). His pain is real, but he brings it to the Lord and relies on *his* unfailing love and faithfulness (verses 4, 8–9). The psalmist is confident that God hears and answers, just as the centurion and widow were to discover centuries later. He is a God of both wrath and mercy (verses 1–2), but a later psalm develops this truth and reminds us he is slow to act on the first, and abounding in the other (Psalm 103:8). If you are crying 'How long?' this evening, know that he hears you and meditate on verse 9 as you end the day.

DOUBTING

READ: LUKE 7:18–35

> *John the Baptist sent us to you to ask, 'Are you the one*
> *who is to come, or should we expect someone else?'*
>
> LUKE 7:20

Doubting is part of discipleship. It is not the same as unbelief. The English word comes from the word '*double*': it is about being caught in two minds about something. And the reason Christians can find themselves caught in two minds is because we have to live in two worlds: the world of the kingdom of God, with its promises and assurances – a world of hope, joy, peace and justice; and the world we actually inhabit – one of 24/7 news, wars and rumours of wars, ecological catastrophe, racial tension, heightened crime. This latter world mocks our faith and causes us to ask ourselves, 'Is it real? Am I believing a fairy story?'

There are at least two poignant stories of doubters in the Gospels. The most famous features Thomas in John 20, and we can have a lot of sympathy with him because he was being asked to believe in something unheard of, unprecedented – resurrection! But, in today's passage there is a different type of doubter, John the Baptist, and this story perhaps resonates even more with our experiences.

John is in prison (see Matthew 11:2–3) and although he was close to Jesus, as his cousin who had prophesied about him and baptized him (see Luke 3), it was hard for John to see beyond his circumstances, to look beyond his chains – and so he starts to doubt and wants answers from Jesus. Note the *double* mind behind the question:

'Are you the one who is to come, *or* shall we look for another?' (verse 20, ESV, my emphasis).

Sometimes doubts arise out of intellectual struggling, and sometimes they come because we are facing a significant temptation and looking for a way to have both what we want *and* still remain a disciple (not possible, by the way)! However, often doubts arise in the midst of extreme hardship and suffering when we cry out and ask God if he is really there. If that was true of John, whom Jesus describes as the greatest of the prophets (verses 26–28), then we should not be surprised if it happens to us. But if we follow John in his doubting, we should also follow him in how he sought answers to his doubts.

The right question

Notice that John asked the right question. He was open about his doubts; he was vulnerable. He didn't care how it looked that he, the great prophet whom people had flocked to see (verses 24–26), didn't have all the answers and might be having a crisis of faith. This was too important to play games or keep up appearances, so he asks 'are you the one?' (verse 20). This is the fundamental question for any disciple. Do we follow because he is indeed the *only* one, because there is no other hope, no other truth? John needed that question resolved.

The right person

John also asked the right person; he went straight to the source. How often have we seen doubters turn to other places for satisfaction or temporary answers or to other people to affirm their doubts – to tell them what they want to hear? John went straight to Jesus. Did Jesus answer? Well, maybe not in the way we would expect, but he reminded him of the evidence, and he did so by referring to Isaiah, a passage that John would have known by heart and which we looked at a few days ago in Luke 4.

The deliberate omission

But Jesus leaves something out. If you look at Luke 4:18 and compare it to what Jesus says to John, you will see that he mentions the poor and the blind, but he omits the phrase about *setting the prisoners free* – the very phrase of most relevance to John! But John would know what Jesus was doing. Jesus was encouraging John not to 'fall away' (see verse 23) even though he found himself in prison. The Puritan preacher Richard Baxter found himself in prison, but his personal circumstances did not stop the truth from being true. Freedom was coming.

At the IFES World Assembly in South Africa, I remember a short drama piece based on this story by Tom de Craene, the leader of the Flemish Belgian movement. In it, when John's disciples return, they report back what Jesus has said. Clutching the bars of his cell, John notices the omission from Isaiah 61 and asks: 'Did he say anything about the captives?' 'No,' they reply, 'But he is setting people free.'

We may feel that there are many things God is *not* doing to help us in our current situation, but when we begin to look outside of our own 'momentary troubles', as Paul calls them, to the 'eternal glory' in store for us (2 Corinthians 4:17), we can see what he *is* doing: changing lives, giving vision, healing hearts, bringing freedom.

Cousin John was close to Jesus, but anyone who has experienced the tiniest piece of God's grace is closer (verse 28) because we are now the brothers and sisters of Christ through the freedom bought for us on the cross

(Luke 8:21; Romans 8:16–17). The path of doubt can lead us back to the highway of faith strengthened, reaffirmed and wiser. As Jesus concludes his mini sermon to those who had listened in to his conversation with John's disciples, he uses a proverb that essentially means that true wisdom is seen in its fruits. The doubter who works through those doubts in the light of God's revelation is, in the end, wiser than those who never doubt their own goodness and righteousness (verse 35).

PRAY:

> Lord, take my doubts and answer the cry of my heart. Show me more of you today: more of your truth, more of your grace. Open my eyes to look beyond my own personal prison and see where you are at work in the world. Help me not to fall away but keep me secure in your arms and grounded on your Word, I pray. Amen.

THE WIDER STORY

READ: LUKE 8:22 – 9:9

Chapter 8:22–56 shows Jesus' power over nature, over the demonic and over death itself. In Chapter 9:1–6, Jesus starts delegating his ministry and authority, giving his disciples their first 'mission experience'. As his ministry becomes more public this brings hostility from those who felt threatened by him, and we read in Chapter 9:7–9 the sad news that John did not experience deliverance in this life, but also that his death brought no peace to his murderer. Herod now had to deal with a much greater power.

REFLECT:

- Which of these stories of Jesus' authority (over the natural environment and the powers of darkness, sickness and death) brings you the greatest assurance today? Why?
- How can John's story help us to keep an eternal perspective when it comes to persecution or suffering?

AN EVENING PSALM

READ: PSALM 31

John the Baptist could have meditated on many of the words of this psalm while he was in prison. Verses 9–13 describe a broken man, but this lament is framed by two longer important sections, and this prevents him from lapsing into despair. In verses 1–8 the psalmist describes God as his rock and his refuge, and in faith he expresses his trust in God and recognizes what God has done for him (verses 5–8). Then, in verses 14 onwards, he confesses his faith in the God who rescues. Verse 14 repeats verse 6 'I trust', and 'refuge' is mentioned again in verse 19. While he prays fervently to be delivered (verses 16–18), the whole psalm is one of quiet trust. 'My times are in your hands' he affirms (verse 15), and then concludes, 'Be strong and take heart' (verse 24), words spoken to himself and 'all … who hope in the LORD'. Like the psalmist, like John, let us leave our days in the hands of God and make verses 23–24 our prayer tonight.

WHO'S FEEDING YOU?

READ: LUKE 9:10–27

> *They all ate and were satisfied, and the disciples picked up twelve basketfuls of broken pieces that were left over.*
>
> LUKE 9:17

This is the only miracle recorded in all four Gospels, possibly because of the sheer scale of what was involved in providing so much out of so little, but more likely because of its importance in demonstrating the nature of the kingdom that Jesus was bringing in.

Tasters of the eternal kingdom

For a special birthday treat, my wife Gwen once bought me a 'tasting meal' at a well-known restaurant; she knows I find choosing from a menu difficult! The advantage of a tasting menu is that you are served a sample of all their best dishes in one evening. It is a feast.

The ministry of Jesus, as recorded in the Gospels, is essentially a 'tasting menu' for the kingdom of heaven. Here and now, we get glimpses of what heaven is like: sickness is gone, evil is denounced, death is dispelled, sins are forgiven. In this case, the hungry are satisfied. Jesus nourishes and satisfies his people. We have already heard his mother prophesy this in her song (Luke 1:53).

In many of his parables Jesus uses the image of a feast to describe the final kingdom (see also Revelation 19:9). The 5,000 mentioned here foreshadow the 144,000 in heaven which was a symbolic number for a crowd that 'no one could count' (Revelation 7:9). Every encounter with Jesus we experience is a taster of the kingdom to come. Every moment of peace in the storm, light in the darkness, joy amidst sorrow, love when we are brokenhearted, truth spoken into our doubts, is an anticipation of kingdom peace, light, joy, love and truth in all its fullness.

The compassionate provider

In Mark's account of this miracle he mentions Christ's compassion for his listeners (Mark 6:34). This compassion motivated Christ both to teach and feed them. He could not have let this crowd go hungry when they had sacrificed so much time and energy just to come and listen to him. It was a supreme demonstration of his love and power in perfect harmony. He who had refused to turn stones into bread for his own use (Luke 4:3–4), had no hesitation in using his power lovingly to provide for those in need.

We never outgrow our dependence on him

Jesus himself foretold that there would be those who would turn away from following him (Luke 8:13; Matthew 13:21). It is always sad to watch this happening and there are many reasons people give to explain why they no longer follow Christ. However, perhaps the one that makes least sense is when people claim they 'outgrew their faith'.

The Christian life is a marathon, not a sprint. So, as we grow in our understanding and experience, as our faith deepens, we may recognize that some things which were once 'black and white' are actually more complex. Nevertheless, we can never outgrow our faith, or our utter dependence on Christ. In fact, the further we go on the Christian journey, the more dependent we realize we are as the Holy Spirit chips away at our pride and self-sufficiency.

Jesus' words to the disciples in verse 13 appear a little unfair – challenging at least! Just before this miracle the disciples were amazed that they were able to perform some of the miracles that Jesus himself had done (verse 6). The same thing happens in the following chapter (10:17). However, we come to see that this had the potential to become a source of pride (9:46–48). And so, by asking them to provide the food, Jesus reminds them that they can only do what *he* empowers them to do (see 9:40). In his guide to prayer, Jesus teaches them – and us – to pray for daily bread (11:3). From the most basic (food) to the most spectacular (exorcisms and healings), the message of the passage is that *he* is the one who powerfully provides. However he chooses to answer our prayers, he will give us much more than we could ever imagine.

The baskets left over (verse 17) teach us that God is never short of resources. It is madness to try to 'go it alone' in our discipleship or ministry. This will inevitably result in failure and disappointment. But if we rely increasingly on him, we will not only be satisfied, there will be an abundance for others as well. Think of the ways in which you might be tempted to doubt God's provision or become focused on what you lack, rather than what he can give.

PRAY:

Lord Jesus, thank you for promising to feed me, both physically and spiritually. Prevent me from failing to trust you for the basic essentials of life or from greedily hoarding for myself. Nourish me by your Word and each day give me tasters of your kingdom. I pray for those I know who have wandered from you and tried to 'go it alone'. Help me to depend on you continually and never think I can do it on my own strength. In Jesus' name I pray, Amen.

THE WIDER STORY

READ: LUKE 9:28–42

Luke 9:28–42 tells the story of a mountain and a valley. In verses 28–36 we have the story of the transfiguration, then in 37–42 there is the contrasting story of 'life in the real world' as Jesus is confronted with the demonic and heals a young lad. The ineffectiveness of the disciples (verse 40) and the amazement of the crowd (verse 43) continue two themes from today's readings.

REFLECT:

- Some of us may tend towards waiting for the next 'mountaintop' experience of the deep presence of God; some of us may tend towards constant discouragement at the power of evil around us. How do these stories help us navigate living in the kingdom of God *and* in a broken world?
- In verse 43 the crowds were 'astonished at the majesty of God' (ESV). When were you last astonished at his majesty? Take time to reflect on how, even in a world of demons, his majesty can still be discovered.

AN EVENING PSALM

READ: PSALM 23

This is probably the most famous of the Psalms. There is something about the image of the shepherd and his care for his stubborn, wandering sheep that transcends cultures and languages. It is simple in what it is saying and yet profound in what it tells us about God and the depth of his care. He provides everything for us (verse 1); he guides us to a good place and gives us nourishment and rest (verses 2–3); he protects us and comforts us in our darkest hours (verse 4); he raises us up and his spiritual blessings are more than we can think or imagine (verse 5).

The final verse is worth special attention. Very often we think of goodness being something that we have to achieve or pursue, but the image here is of God's goodness and mercy pursuing *us* all the days of our life, until eventually we arrive at home. It is as if he won't let us get away – like the shepherd, he will pursue his sheep until he guides them safely in to their pen. This morning we watched as Jesus fed his people. In Mark's account of that miracle (Mark 6:30 and the following verses) we read that Jesus had compassion on the crowd 'because they were like sheep without a shepherd' (Mark 6:34). So what does he do? He leads them to a green pasture and gets them to rest there (Mark 6:39) before satisfying them with more food than they could eat (Mark 6:42–43).

Our God is generous. His resources are inexhaustible; his kingdom is one of abundance! When Christ fed the multitude in Galilee and the baskets overflowed, he was giving a picture of the great final banquet to which this psalm also looks forward. Read Psalm 23 again slowly and meditate on the many ways God has been your provider, your comforter and your guide.

PRIDE & PREJUDICE

READ: LUKE 9:43–56; 10:25–37

*Which of these three do you think was a neighbour
to the man who fell into the hands of robbers?*

LUKE 10:36

The Gospels never airbrush out the faults or imperfections
of the characters. This is especially true of the disciples.
These are not the haloed holy figures that stare down at
us from statues or stained-glass windows. These are real
people and in today's reading we see personality clashes,
arguments and sectarian hatred. There are four stories
that feature in today's readings.

Story 1: Spiritual pride

We don't know what sparked the argument. Perhaps
three of them were still on a spiritual high after the
mountaintop experience of Luke 9:28–36, and the rest
were on a spiritual low after their failure of verses 37–40.
Perhaps the three were looking down on the others –
we know that James and John certainly had ambitions
(Matthew 20:20–21). Pride is not just crass boasting
about our own achievements. We can also be proud of
our piety, our ministry successes, our 'spiritual' gifts,
and when that happens it is all the more harmful. It
turns our successes into failures and in the eyes of God
it diminishes whatever we have achieved because we
have forgotten the most important thing: *love* (see 1
Corinthians 13:1).

What is most disturbing about the disciples' attitude is that it comes after Jesus tells them he is going to die (verses 43–45). Arguing over who is the greatest is pathetic and ugly at any time, but here their sense of timing is abysmal. They have so much to learn. Instead of showing their love and devotion to Jesus and committing to learn more from him, they break his heart.

Story 2: Pointless competitiveness

But the disciples were not just proud – they were prejudiced. They tried to stop someone else's 'Jesus ministry' simply because 'he is not one of us' (verse 49). Today, we might hear similar words to the tune of 'he isn't a member of our church!' But Jesus makes it clear that there is no room for such attitudes in the kingdom of God. The disciples needed to learn what Paul taught years later in Philippians 1:18 – that even if we don't like someone, or have doubts about their motives, if they are telling people about Jesus then we should rejoice and leave it to God.

Story 3: Cultural prejudice

Their prejudice takes a whole new turn, however, in Luke 9:51–56. Our world is such a tapestry of war and international conflict that, wherever you are reading this, you can probably easily think of a historic enemy: maybe a country, or a community within your own country that you do not like, or whom you find it hard to trust. For the disciples, that was Samaria – and it was mutual. The aggressive response of the Samaritans pressed all the wrong buttons for James and John who fancied themselves as modern-day 'Elijahs' (see 2 Kings 1) and wanted to use divine resources to destroy a whole community. But Jesus rebukes them. In some manuscripts and versions his words are quoted as: 'You do not know what manner of spirit you are of. For the Son of Man did not come to destroy men's lives, but to save them' (verses 55–56, NKJV).

The disciples were learning that in this new kingdom there was no place for pride, prejudice or hatred. Later they would learn first-hand what 'Spirit' they had, and John would see fire come down (see Acts 2:3–4), but not as he expected. He would see even the Samaritans filled with the same Holy Spirit (Acts 8:14–17).

Story 4: Surprising grace

Since even his closest disciples harboured this intense hatred for Samaritans, Jesus uses a conversation in the next chapter to tell the story, not about the bad Samaritans who closed their borders to him, but of a 'Good Samaritan' who showed up the heartlessness of the Jewish religious leaders and helped a man in distress. The story was prompted by a question based on the Law of 'love your neighbour as yourself' (Leviticus 19:18). Jesus was asked: 'Who is my neighbour?' (verse 29). But the question shows that the questioner was not interested in the answer. His real question was: 'Can you define "neighbour" for me, so that I can know who I *don't* have to love?'

And so, Jesus tells a story which makes it clear that everyone, including your despised enemy, is your neighbour. And he turns it round. It is not a Jew showing amazing grace by helping one of these unlovable Samaritans; it is a Samaritan showing more love than the most pious of Jews. When Jesus finishes by saying, 'Go and do likewise' (verse 37), he knows he is setting an impossible task. Left to our natural instincts none of us can really display such love. But he doesn't ask that of us. He gives us a different Spirit and, as he predicted in verses 43–45, he himself demonstrated just what love for our enemies *really* looks like: 'But God demonstrates his own love for us in this: while we were still sinners, Christ died for us' (Romans 5:8).

PRAY:

> *Lord, this passage challenges me so much. Forgive me for the times I have been jealous of others and tried to make myself big at their expense; forgive me for the times I have resented the ministry of other churches or groups, and spoken harshly of them; forgive me for the times I have harboured sectarian or racist thoughts about others. Help me to understand how big your heart is for all people and to rely on you to raise me to levels of love that I could never achieve in my own strength. Amen.*

THE WIDER STORY

READ: LUKE 9:57–62; 10:38 – 11:54

Luke 9:57–62 records three short encounters with Jesus by 'would-be disciples', and exposes the things that were holding them back. Then, after the parable of the Samaritan who helped the needy, we have the story of Jesus who seems to be rebuking his friend Martha – for helping! (10:38–42). But this story demonstrates that 'helping' is not an absolute. Sometimes there is a place for being still and listening. Serving Jesus should never be at the expense of listening to Jesus. This is why Chapter 11 contains his teaching on prayer, including the famous 'Lord's Prayer' (verses 1–13). The rest of the chapter is about spiritual warfare, whether it be the demonic (verses 14–28) or the more subtle unbelief of the religious leaders who should know better (verses 37–54), and who on Judgment Day will be shown up by the outsiders they despised (verses 29–32; see also 10:13–15). At heart, this is a battle between light and darkness (verses 33–36).

REFLECT:

- What do you think lay behind the response of Jesus in Luke 9:57–62? How does it challenge our discipleship?
- It is often said: 'Serving Jesus should never be at the expense of listening to Jesus.' Reflect on how your desire to do things *for* Jesus might be stopping you from listening *to* Jesus.
- How can the teaching in Chapter 11 make us more fervent in prayer?
- Can you see in yourself any of the things that Jesus rebuked the Pharisees for (11:37–46)? In what way(s)? Pray that these would disappear as you spend time listening to Jesus through his Word.

AN EVENING PSALM

READ: PSALM 131

This is one of the 'road songs' that the pilgrims would have sung on their procession to Jerusalem to worship. It is a psalm of perspective, a reminder of who we are in the 'grand scheme of things' (verse 1). Our morning reading was about another walk to Jerusalem (Luke 9:51–52); one where the disciples were bickering, full of pride and self-importance. They should have been meditating on this psalm. It is not just a psalm of humility; it is a psalm of trust and contentment (verse 2). There are few greater images of peacefulness than a weaned child with its mother. In contrast to a feeding baby fussing at the mother's breast, a weaned child is often content just to be with her. The child feels safe and secure knowing and trusting her for everything, That is why this short psalm ends with the pilgrims reminding each other to stay close to God, the place of intimacy where they are safe and secure, and to be content that he will supply all their needs.

Take time to slowly read and reflect on these verses. Confess your pride and express your desire to stay close to God and trust him completely. Place your hope in him as you look forward to the days ahead.

MISSION IMPOSSIBLE?

READ: LUKE 10:1–24

Go! I am sending you out like lambs among wolves.
LUKE 10:3

Here, and in Matthew 10, we see the first two short-term mission teams. Jesus gives these disciples a taste of what it will be like in the future to go on mission with him. There are some clear similarities and differences in terms of how we may engage in specific concentrated times of mission today. In terms of differences, there are instructions which applied specifically to that context (verse 4), and there is the reality that the missionaries' knowledge both of Jesus and the message of his kingdom was extremely limited. Unlike us today, they had neither the gospel of salvation nor a full understanding of Jesus' identity or why he had come. They were simply told to preach that 'the kingdom of God has come near' (verse 9). But there were some elements of this proto-mission trip that still apply to our call to mission today.

Preparing the way for Jesus

They were to go to the places where Jesus himself was shortly to visit (verse 1) and they were to model his ministry and preach the coming of the kingdom (verses 8–9). They were like the advance party that sets up the tents for a festival or goes ahead of a band on tour to have the stage ready. They were to have a future perspective; the focus was not to be on them but on the one who was to come (see also verse 20). Our mission is the same: to prepare the way for Jesus. At one level, our witness, our testimonies, our proclamation, our apologetics are the means God uses by his Spirit to prepare the ground of people's hearts for him to come and change them. At another level, our mission today is carried out in the light of Jesus' return (see Acts 1:10–11) as we preach that the kingdom has come and that we all need to be ready for when the master, Jesus, returns.

Being prepared for opposition

Jesus is realistic in his instructions. This is hardly the typical pre-match locker room pep talk. He tells his fledgling missionaries that they will be like 'lambs among wolves' (verse 3) and that many will not listen to their message (verse 16). Some Christian mission preparation talks I have heard owe more to the locker room than to the Bible; peppered as they are with back-slapping, hyped-up 'we can take this world for Jesus' sound bites rather than the more sobering recognition that spiritually we fight a formidable enemy and cannot enter the battle carelessly or arrogantly. In the battle there will be discouragement, misrepresentation and mockery; we may be tempted to think that our mission is pointless and our faith is a lie. At these times we need to recognize that those voices are simply the enemy, Satan's propaganda gatecrashing our spiritual frequency. The source is satanic (see verses 18–19). We need to be prepared for this reality.

Being prayerful and confident in Christ

Being realistic and having a healthy respect for the opposition is not the same as lacking confidence. It is a question of where our confidence is placed. Jesus' words before and after this mission trip remind us that the mission is *his* and the outcome is assured. The whole trip is book-ended with prayer. In verse 2 he tells the disciples to pray for missionaries to go; in the next verse they become the missionaries. Afterwards, in verse 21 Jesus utters a prayer of praise to his Father. All mission can only survive on the oxygen of prayer. Throughout the passage there is a theme of vulnerability. The disciples are to pray because they are vulnerable (verse 2); lambs among wolves are vulnerable (verse 3); they are to take no unnecessary props with them because they are to stay vulnerable (verse 4); when they cannot foresee the response they will get to their message they will remain vulnerable (verses 5–12). But it is this very vulnerability which can breed confidence for all of us who follow these disciples into mission – because it is not us who are defeating the powers of darkness, it is Christ.

While they were out proclaiming, healing and exorcising, Jesus says he saw Satan falling (verses 18–19). Every piece of kingdom ministry is another nail in Satan's coffin. The world may see a student reading the Bible with a flatmate, or befriending and offering hospitality in the name of Christ to an international student, but Jesus sees Satan falling. The world may see a believer campaigning for justice in the name of Christ, or proclaiming the uniqueness of Jesus and the hope of the resurrection to a sceptical audience, but Jesus sees Satan falling. We may think we are offering words of counsel, or simply kneeling to help someone pray for forgiveness and grace, but Jesus sees Satan falling.

All of this is cause for confidence and rejoicing, yet Jesus cautions us that we are never to rejoice in what we have achieved lest we start to gain our identity and sense of worth from our ministry – from what *we* do. Rather, we are to rejoice that our 'names are written in heaven' (verse 20); that is, we are to rejoice, not in what we are doing for Christ, but in what *he* has done for us! We rejoice that he loved us enough to find a way of ensuring that our names would be on the heavenly roll of citizens.

A student story

Many of the European movements have been pioneered or strengthened through short-term mission teams from other countries: such as Montenegro's 'Camp Monty' (a personal favourite!) assisted by students from Denmark and elsewhere in the Balkans; or several Eurasian countries who have benefitted from English camps facilitated by students from the United Kingdom. In other regions, Cambodia has received students from Singapore, and in Ghana, some graduates have gone to more remote areas of their own country to pioneer ministry in high schools. Often these experiences are as significant for the people going on mission as they are for those receiving.

The disciples learned more about the character of the kingdom of God as they went out on mission. Similarly, one student from the Singaporean team honestly reflected on his Cambodia experience: 'I was overwhelmed by the many things that you have to consider, to give up and to invest in order to win people for Christ.'

While these disciples had a positive mission experience, we know so much more. If Jesus was able to remind them that they had far more knowledge and privileges than even David or Elijah (verse 24), how much more do we have – since we know how this story ends and how much it cost Christ to ensure that our names were on that list?

PRAY:

> *Lord, help me to see my life with you as a mission. I ask you to help me prepare a way for you among those I come into contact with each day. Thank you for revealing how this story ends and preparing me for the reality of opposition. Help me not to be distracted by hype or discouragement but prayerfully to play my part in answering the call to mission, that your kingdom might come. Amen.*

THE WIDER STORY

READ: LUKE 12:1 – 13:9

Chapter 12:1–12 warns that opposition from religious leaders to the gospel of Jesus will be inevitable (14:1–6 tells of the same conflict). In between, there are various stories about judgment, beginning with 12:13–34 – an illustration of God's judgment over a 'rich fool' and a warning against the power of money. Continuing the theme of judgment, Chapter 12:35–59 paints a picture of Jesus' second coming as judge and emphasizes the need to be ready (13:1–5) and to show signs of fruitfulness (13:6–9), otherwise we too may perish when our time comes.

REFLECT:

- What does the parable of the rich man tell us about the power and destructiveness of ambition which is centred on wealth?
- What in Luke 12 can help us guard against the dangerous temptations of ambition and anxiety?
- How can the teaching on 'readiness' (verses 35 and

the following verses) make us more spiritually alert at times of division and hostility?

- How can Luke 13:1–5 help us to understand the proper response to the tragic events that occur daily in our world?

AN EVENING PSALM

READ: PSALM 126

This psalm remembers what it was like to have your dreams come true (verse 1) and it is a prayer that God would do it again (verse 4). It belongs to the period at the very end of the Old Testament after the people of Israel have returned from exile in Babylon. This would have happened perhaps a generation before, but now they are settled into the humdrum of life back in a land where things are still economically and politically difficult, and it is a short step from discouragement to spiritual disillusionment. The psalmist prays against this. He wants the people to laugh again, to sing again. He wants the reputation of God and his people to be restored (verse 2).

The end of the psalm reminds us of this morning's reading. The fear and vulnerability with which the disciples would have gone out, was followed by a joyful return as they saw the fruit of their harvest (compare verse 6 and Luke 10:2, 17). Is there any area of your life or ministry where you feel that you are 'sowing in tears'? Can you recall times when your spiritual life was full of laughter and joy? Pray that you will reap with joy. Sentimental nostalgia keeps us stuck in the past, but holy nostalgia reminds us of the goodness and character of God and gives us the boldness to ask him to 'do it again'.

COUNTING THE COST

READ: LUKE 14:7–35

> *Whoever does not carry their cross and follow me*
> *cannot be my disciple.*
>
> LUKE 14:27

I remember accidentally 'gatecrashing' a party. A friend misunderstood an invitation and some of us showed up when the hosts weren't expecting us. It was awkward and it was soon very clear that we didn't fit into the evening's plans. Many people think they wouldn't be welcome into the Christian community. They would feel like uninvited guests. They're not 'the religious type'. Sadly, Christians may give that impression – accidentally or even intentionally. But it is not the Jesus way.

Gatecrashers welcome

We saw how, when Jesus fed the 5,000, it was a taster for the heavenly feast, and this section of Luke's Gospel is where we find many of those 'feast' or 'banquet stories' (see also Luke 13:29–30). Here, as he eats at a Pharisee's house, Jesus talks again about a feast. In the first two stories, he shows the upside-down values of his kingdom. The last are first. It is like a wedding reception where the ones on the periphery, who think they barely know the bride and groom, are invited to sit with them at the top table (Luke 14:7–11). It's like a royal official distributing invitations to the king's palace around the homeless shelters (verses 12–14). There are no gatecrashers; everyone is invited, everyone 'fits in' here. Is it any wonder that one of Jesus' companions said, in effect: Blessed is anyone invited to that party (see verse 15)?

Excuses not welcome

Then Jesus uses it as an opportunity to expand the story a little (verses 16–24), and focus not just on those who are invited but also those who missed out. Although his co-diner clearly thought this was a party you wouldn't want to miss, Jesus gives him a reality check and shows how easy it is for some people to find reasons to refuse his hospitality. None of the excuses (verses 18–20) are remotely believable: you don't buy property without seeing it; you don't buy a car without test-driving it; and no host would invite a newly married man without also inviting his wife. In this culture a feast was about more than the food; it was about being accepted into the community, even into the wider family of the host.

The truth was that these various invitees – representing the temptations of wealth, status and relationships – preferred the company of their lovers, their land, and even their beasts to the company of the king. They were offered great food and even greater company but their hearts were so small and their imaginations so limited that they would prefer to stand and stare at a field.

For those who do not want to follow Jesus there will be no shortage of excuses available, but they can be reduced to a common root: they are in love with something else and are not prepared to give it up – not even for the best of invitations! Meanwhile there will always be those only too happy to accept Jesus' generous and gracious invitation to his table.

Count the cost

In some ways, those who refused got something right. They had done a quick calculation and decided it wasn't worth it. That is why Luke follows this story with the teaching on the cost of being a disciple (verses 25–33).

A young friend of mine had become a Christian and her unsympathetic parents resented that she now spent Sunday mornings worshipping rather than out walking with them. Even though she had not reduced the time she spent with them in total – just reapportioned it – they didn't understand and asked her one weekend, 'Why do you suddenly hate us so much?' It was nonsense of course. She loved her parents deeply, but the fact that Jesus was now the greatest object of her affections meant that in their self-absorbed state they interpreted her new priorities as hatred.

That is the context of Jesus' hard words (verses 25–27). It is as if Jesus is saying: 'So be it, if you are not willing for your love for me to be interpreted as "hate" by those closest to you, then this is probably not the life for you.' The invitation to his banquet is free – but it is not cheap. It involves leaving many things behind – even people – because, although we want to continue nurturing friendships, very often those friends will not be able to cope with our new priorities.

A student story

Many of the students I have met know first-hand the cost of following Jesus. I remember as a pastor once helping a student whose atheistic parents withdrew a lot of privileges from him until he 'gave up this religious nonsense and concentrated on his career' like his older brother. For others, there is even more at stake. One Asian student, who came to Christ in Ireland and was baptized, left one summer to return home. He felt compelled to tell his father that he was now a Christian, knowing that his father had the power and authority to withhold the finances needed for his studies, meaning he risked never returning and never finishing his degree. However, his Irish student friends prayed fervently for him and his family all summer and celebrated when he returned and told of his father's 'miraculous' change in attitude. For others it is not a happy ending, but they regard it as a price worth paying.

So count the cost, the same way a military general or a property developer would. It impacts not just our family relationships but also how we view our own life (verse 26). Anyone in Palestine who was paraded through the streets carrying their cross was about to be nailed to it. Half-hearted devotion is of no use to Jesus; just as flavourless salt is of no use. But of course, he asks us to do nothing that he hasn't *first* done for us – and more. We die to ourselves because *he* has already died for us; we hate the substandard life we try to make for ourselves because *he* has promised us a far greater life (John 10:10); we carry our cross for him because *he first* carried his cross for us.

PRAY:

> *Thank you for inviting me to the feast, Jesus! Often I feel like the invitation was sent to the wrong address or that I am not wearing appropriate clothes for the party. But then I remember that you have welcomed the poor and the homeless, the unloved and the distant relations. Even in my humble state, I can sit with you at the feast. I pray that I would always*

welcome 'the last and the least'. Help me also to
prioritize you above everything and to count the
cost, knowing that whatever sacrifices I make for
you, you are worth it! Amen.

THE WIDER STORY

READ: LUKE 13:10 – 14:6

Many aspects of the kingdom cannot be seen now
(verses 18–21). Some of what we think we see may be
false, as God judges hypocrisy. The upside-down nature
of the kingdom is seen in Luke 13:30. In verses 10–17 he
judges the religious leaders for their lack of compassion,
while his heart was full of compassion even for those
who rejected him (verses 31–35).

REFLECT:

- What do the illustrations of the mustard seed, dough
  and narrow door tell us about the kingdom of God?
  How could that encourage us when little growth may
  appear to be happening in our lives or ministry?
- Reflect on Jesus' response to Herod's schemes and
  his heart for the city who rejected him. Why was he
  so determined to go to Jerusalem, knowing what lay
  ahead of him?

AN EVENING PSALM

READ: PSALM 68:1–18

English poet GM Hopkins wrote that 'the world is charged with the grandeur of God'[1] and Psalm 68 tells the same story. It is a story of God's power (verses 1–2) and majesty (verse 4). He is the cosmic, victorious king showering blessings on his people (verses 7–9) and conquering their oppressors (verses 11–14). Even the most majestic sights of nature are eclipsed by his power and beauty (verses 15–17). But hand in hand with this power and majesty is the repeated statement that he is a compassionate God who cares for the orphans and widows, the lonely, the oppressed and the poor (verses 5, 6, 10). In this morning's reading, Jesus reflects his Father's heart when he commands us to invite the poor, the blind and the lame into the kingdom. Paul applies verse 18 to the spiritual gifts we have received from this victorious God (Ephesians 4:8). We can therefore 'be glad and rejoice' (verse 3) since we have been made righteous by Christ. Read this psalm again, in the light of verse 3, giving thanks for the victories God has won for you in Jesus.

1 Gerard Manley Hopkins, 'God's Grandeur' in *Gerard Manley Hopkins: The Major Works* (Oxford University Press, 2009), p128.

LOST & FOUND

READ: LUKE 15:1–32

> *In the same way, I tell you, there is rejoicing in the*
> *presence of the angels of God over one sinner who*
> *repents.*
>
> LUKE 15:10

How frustrating it can be to lose something really important (your car keys or phone) or how sickening it can be to lose something really valuable (a piece of jewellery handed down to you by your grandmother)! How chilling it can be to read or hear that a person has gone missing, especially if it is someone you know or a young child! We all know the dangers of being lost. Jesus uses the image of 'lostness' to describe humanity separated from its creator (Luke 19:10). Part of his ministry was to bring us home to where we belong.

There are many ways to be lost

Jesus tells three parables about being lost. The first item is the coin, mislaid and needing to be discovered; the second is the sheep which has accidentally wandered off and needs to be rescued; the third is the son who willfully runs away and wants to be lost in terms of his relationship to his father. All of these are true of us. We are lost on many different levels. Like the coin, we begin our story separated from our owner – we are, by nature, lost to God because of our sin (Romans 3:23; Ephesians 2:1–2, 12). Like the sheep, perhaps unconsciously, we have wandered away – simply following our own desires and not even realizing that they take us far away from God. And like the son, there are times when we have willfully and deliberately turned our back on God and wanted to remove ourselves far from him. Ultimately, the reason we have turned away from God doesn't matter; in each and every case, we are still lost.

There's only one way to be found

All of these stories (well, almost all) have a happy ending. The coin, the sheep and the son are found. In the first two stories, represented by the woman and the shepherd, God actively pursues and searches for the lost item; in the third, he patiently waits and watches for the wanderer to come home, and when he sees him (still a long distance away), he runs out to welcome him. We are not found until God the Father finds us and welcomes us. There is no other home, except back in his sheepfold, or under his roof, accepting his hospitality (notice the image of the feast again, verse 23). As the father waited patiently at the window it is as if his webcam is permanently set to watching the driveway; his email and mobile notifications are permanently on waiting for that message 'I'm coming home.'

It comes at a cost. You may be familiar with some old depictions of this story – I used to see them in churches – featuring a serene Jesus looking like he has stepped out of a shower, holding a fluffy lamb on his shoulders. Then I saw something much more realistic, actually a cartoon drawing in a children's Bible! It showed the shepherd with torn robes and tousled hair, with blood on his face and arms from the thorns and briars, dragging a 'sheepish-looking sheep' back to the fold. When a sheep got lost, it was almost certainly in trouble: in a pit or caught in thorn bushes. The rescue operation cost the blood, sweat and tears of the shepherd. *That's* the realistic picture. The story of our rescue is a story of a bruised and bloodied shepherd enduring thorns and nails, to lay down his life for his undeserving sheep (see John 10:11).

Don't miss the party

But there is actually a fourth way to be lost. And this is the story that doesn't have a happy ending. Jesus told these stories because he had been criticized by the religious hierarchy for the company he was keeping (verse 2). So at the end of the three parables he tells us about the second son: the one who tried to earn his father's love by duty and hard work, but who couldn't understand the father's grace or comprehend the bigness of his heart. He lived by merit and thought he deserved the father's love – just like the people in verse 2. Yet at the end of the story he is outside, missing out on the party. While the younger son's rebellion and sin did not exclude him, the older son's self-righteousness did – because he believed that confession and repentance were too humiliating for him. The younger son knew he didn't deserve to be in the father's house; the older son's sense of entitlement led him to question his father's judgment, even his morality.

We can be lost by running away from God, but we can also be lost by staying where we are, doing religious things and relating to God on our terms. Being religious can be as dangerous as being irreligious. The anger of the older son towards this loving, gracious father shows that, throughout the whole story, the older son was as lost as the younger one. By closing his heart to grace and standing on the doorstep, the older son was as far away from the father as the younger son was when he was in the faraway country. The father loved both sons equally.

He pleads with the older one to come in, but we don't know if he actually did. The story is left open for the religious leaders to make the choice. But the chances are, they missed the party.

PRAY:

> *Lord, in your love you have pursued and found me, not, as some might say: 'I have found God'. Help me to live in the warmth of your embrace, amazed that you sought me out and made me yours. Now that I am safe in your arms, may I never look away to work out the personal cost of being here or to weigh up the right of another to be here too. Instead keep me focused on the sacrifice you made so that I could be yours. Thank you for finding this lost child. Amen.*

THE WIDER STORY

READ: LUKE 16:1 – 18:8

Chapter 16 is made up of two parables about wealth and using it wisely. In the first Jesus observes how even unbelievers know how to use wealth shrewdly. He is not advocating dishonesty, but rather encouraging wisdom (16:10–13), especially since money can be a cruel master. This is brought out in the second story where one man's wealth was acquired at the expense of the poor, and worshipping this wealth eventually led him to hell. Luke 17:1–10 is a warning not to lead others into sin, but rather to always be willing to forgive those who sin against us. There is also a reminder that it is not the size of our faith that matters. Even a little faith can achieve much (verse 6), but our faith or accomplishments should never lead us to think more highly of ourselves than others. We must maintain a servant-heartedness at all times (17:7–10).

Two of Luke's regular concerns – healing, and the outsider – come together in Luke 17:11–19 as Jesus once again travels around Samaria. He heals ten lepers, one of whom was doubly disadvantaged: a leper *and* a Samaritan. Yet it is only this man who returns to worship and thank God. These healings are, of course, signs that the kingdom of God has come, and Jesus teaches more on this theme in verses 20–37. He warns the Pharisees not to be distracted by false claims regarding the kingdom, because it doesn't arrive in ways that can be observed (verse 20) but is already among them. In contrast, he warns his own disciples that once he has gone they are not to be distracted by false messiahs, because when he returns as judge every eye will see him (verse 23 and the following verses). Luke 18:1–8 is a parable about being persistent in prayer, something with which the disciples would continue to struggle (see Luke 22:45).

REFLECT:

- How might these chapters help you to have:
  - A healthy attitude towards money?
  - A biblical concern for the poor?
  - A more humble approach to service?

AN EVENING PSALM

READ: PSALM 119:169–176

Psalm 119 was written to be memorized. All 176 verses! It was slightly easier to do this in the original language of Hebrew because it is divided into 22 sections, each containing 8 verses beginning with consecutive letters of the Hebrew alphabet. One other characteristic is that every single verse contains some reference to the Word of God ('word', 'promise', 'decrees', 'commands' are the first four in this section – verses 169–172). It may seem strange that our first encounter with this psalm is through its final section, but look at the very last verses and you will see the reason. The psalmist finishes his marathon meditation by recognizing his need for the Lord's salvation and sustaining (verses 174–175): he is a lost sheep that the Lord 'seek[s]' (verse 176). Perhaps you are crying out to God, throwing out your prayers to him tonight. Remember that the prayer of verse 176 has been answered in Jesus, the Good Shepherd, who will stop at nothing to rescue those who have wandered away.

TOO PROUD? TOO RICH?

READ: LUKE 18:9–30

Truly I tell you, anyone who will not receive the kingdom of God like a little child will never enter it.

LUKE 18:17

When I was young, if I ever felt that I was no good at something, I would cope by automatically thinking of something different which I was better at. *'Simon may be better at woodwork than I am, but I can play the piano; Joe may be a better swimmer, but I'm on the football team.'* It even crept into my early Christian life: *'Jenny may have got into the worship band, but I've been asked to preach.'* Then, one day at college, I met Ian. No matter what I thought of, it seemed Ian could do it better: he was academically bright, a wizard on the football pitch, he could make the piano sing, and worst of all he was infuriatingly popular with the girls.

The temptation to compare ourselves with others is spiritually disastrous. It may arise out of a sense of inadequacy but it still has its root in envy and it stokes the fires of pride in our heart. It is the sin of our first character in today's reading.

The arrogance of self-sufficiency

Although a parable, the first of Jesus' stories in this passage (verses 9–14) is clearly based on true life. Jesus had encountered many Pharisees and many of the hated political traitors that were tax collectors – and there is no doubt where his sympathies lay. The Pharisees he called 'vipers' and 'hypocrites' (Matthew 12:34; 23:13–29), whereas the repentant tax collectors were welcomed into his kingdom, and two specifically became his followers (see Luke 5:27; 19:1–10).

Luke tells us that this story is specifically aimed at those who were 'confident of their own righteousness and looked down on everyone else' (verse 9). This Pharisee was obsessed with comparisons! His prayer is about himself; God is no more than a captive audience to his own bragging (verses 11–12). This man would never encounter the grace and forgiveness offered by Jesus because he sincerely believed he had no need of it.

The sadness of a divided heart

In contrast, in the third story (verses 18–30) we meet someone (Matthew 19:20 calls him a 'young man') who knew he had a need; that something significant was missing from his life, but he didn't like Jesus' answer. Jesus didn't say that selling everything would earn eternal life; the ruler would still need to follow by committing himself to Jesus in everything (verse 22). What Jesus was doing was putting his finger on the one thing in the ruler's life which meant most to him: the idol of his wealth. The young man was attracted to Jesus' message and wanted what was on offer, but not at any cost. Ultimately, his heart was pulled in another direction. Matthew, when he recounts this story adds a very significant element. He tells us that "he went away sad" (Matthew 19:22). When our heart is divided, meeting Jesus can make us miserable because, if we walk away, clearly we have had a hint of what we are missing.

The humility of utter dependence

If the Pharisee depended on his religion for security, and the young ruler depended on his wealth, in between these stories we see Jesus teaching about the proper posture to adopt if we want a share in the kingdom of God (verses 15–17). The rich young man wanted to 'inherit eternal life' (verse 18) but you don't inherit by *doing*; you inherit by *being* a child of God the Father. A few chapters earlier, Jesus had told his arrogant disciples that they must learn from the little children (Luke 9:46–48; see also Matthew 18:3). It is the posture of utter dependence exhibited by young children that should be the mark of our approach to our heavenly Father. This is, of course, what we see in the other character from the first story.

The honesty of confession

The Pharisee tried to use God, and the things of God, as a means to justify himself. However, the tax collector knew that God could not be used in this way. He had an awareness of God's holiness that the Pharisees, who thought themselves the experts in holiness, could never comprehend. The tax collector brings nothing but his confession; the Pharisee brings his own self-importance and condemnation of others. The Pharisee has a massive issue with being thought a sinner; the tax collector has none, and therefore fulfils all the qualifications for being a disciple. In contrast to the Pharisee who sought God's commendation, he sought God's mercy; in contrast to the young man who went away sad, he goes home justified.

The road of discipleship is not for those in love with themselves or in love with their money. It is for the 'little children' who offer God their undivided hearts and in exchange receive his mercy and grace (verse 17).

PRAY:

> *Lord, as much as I long to be single-minded in following you and faithful in my love for you, I mess up most days. I am reminded of the dangers of self-sufficiency and even being pleased about how well I am doing. Help me to focus on you always and to remember my deep need of your mercy. May I be childlike in my dependence upon you, and mindful of 'whose I am' rather than 'who I am' so that you are at the centre of my life, every hour of every day. Amen.*

THE WIDER STORY

READ: LUKE 18:31 – 19:27

Before the story of Jesus' entry into Jerusalem, Luke tells us of two encounters and a parable. A third prediction of his death (18:31–34) precedes these encounters. We read that the disciples still did not understand what he was saying; that it was 'hidden' from them (verse 34). Ironically, this is immediately followed by a story of Jesus healing the blind (verses 35–43), in line with his manifesto of Luke 4:18 (see also Luke 7:21–22). As Jesus heals many who were physically blind, he is also in the process of opening the eyes of the spiritually blind. Chapter 19 opens with the conversion of yet another outsider: this time a despised tax collector. As a tiny man, collaborating with the Romans and lining his own pockets, Zacchaeus was physically, politically and morally disadvantaged, and yet grace is extended even to him. The people saw him as a sinner (verse 7); Jesus declares him to be part of God's family (verse 9).

The parable of the talents (19:11–27) is a warning that we are to be good stewards of what God has given to us and will be held accountable by God for how we have used his gifts. Better to be a bad steward who has turned good, like Zacchaeus, than those who are privileged in what they have received, like the teachers of the Law, but who are blind to what those Scriptures teach about Jesus.

REFLECT:

- In what ways might we still be 'blind' to who Jesus is and what being a follower of him actually entails?
- How are we stewarding the gifts God has given us?
- How does the story of Zacchaeus encourage us towards daily repentance and generosity?

AN EVENING PSALM

READ: PSALM 49

There are many different types of psalms in Scripture. We're probably familiar with songs of thankfulness and praise, or even lament. But some are what are known as 'wisdom psalms': songs that tell the truth about how life is and how we should live wisely under God. These psalms sound more like passages from the wisdom books such as Ecclesiastes and Proverbs. Psalm 49 is a wisdom psalm. Over half the verses mention wealth or riches. As we saw this morning, one of the biggest discipleship challenges is our attitude to money. Materialism can be spiritually fatal and the recurring theme in this psalm is that wealth counts for nothing when we die. Think of Jesus' words to the rich young man and the sadness of that encounter. If you don't have much wealth you may think that these temptations will not come to you. But that is not true. You can still worship what you don't have! The psalm is addressed to 'rich and poor alike' (verse 2). Pray that God will keep *your* heart from the love of money.

A STRANGE KIND OF KING

READ: LUKE 19:28–44

> *The whole crowd of disciples began joyfully to praise God … 'Blessed is the king who comes in the name of the Lord! Peace in heaven and glory in the highest!'*
>
> LUKE 19:37–38

If you want an example of the meaning of the word 'fickle', I suggest you look at an online forum of football fans after a game. If their team has won, they will be singing the praises of the coach and the players; if they have lost, many of those same fans will be shouting for the manager to be fired, claiming the players are useless and criticizing everyone – from the guys who look after the pitch to those who wash the shirts and drive the team bus! We can all be easily swayed.

The shallowness of the crowd's craving for celebrity

In human terms this was the high point of Jesus' ministry as the crowds gathered to cheer him, but Jesus was not fooled. He was in no danger of believing the hype! He knew that many of these same people would turn against him within a week. Either they would willingly participate or they would stand by and give their silent assent to the cacophony of voices shouting 'crucify him' (Luke 23:21).

However, today they acknowledge his true identity as the king coming in the name of the Lord. This was so true that if the people had not shouted, Jesus says that the stones of the road would have proclaimed it (verse 40). At least stones are reliable and unchanging, not like people. We may think it unusual for a prospective ruler to approach a city on a donkey rather than a warhorse. However, in Jewish history, a donkey could be a symbol of wealth and authority (see Judges 10:3–4; 12:13–14). Likewise, in their religious tradition, while it signified humility and a different model of kingship, it was also to be one of the marks of the coming Messiah (Zechariah 9:9).

The depth of Jesus' compassion

In verses 41–44 Jesus' heart is exposed. He does not harbour bitterness against these fickle people, because among them would be his closest friends. He understood that their eyes were blinded. It would take the extraordinary events of the next ten days, and a lot of suffering, before they would be able to understand what was involved in this 'king' setting up his kingdom.

Jesus: the anti-celebrity

Like the people who lined the streets, we too can allow our personal or political expectations to blind us to the way of the kingdom of God. We can allow our personal agenda of what we would like Jesus to be blind us to who he really is. We can be fickle, praising God one day and turning our backs on him the next. But being a Palm-Sunday-follower is little more than celebrity worship. If Palm Sunday had been the end of the story, Jesus would just have come and gone to be replaced by the next big thing. But his was a mission that no political leader, no earthly king, no celebrity superstar could achieve. It was the way of the cross – the way of rejection, not of popularity

– and that is why it is good to avoid paying attention to how many people are attending the megachurch, or how many followers celebrity pastors have on Twitter, or how many downloads the latest worship songs have; those are the things that impress fickle followers, and they are meaningless; they will pass. God is more interested in why there are people continuing to worship in air raid shelters or refugee camps, still singing as the bullets fly and praying as the bombs fall, trusting – even though they don't know where the next meal is coming from. They do it because, unlike the religious hierarchy of Jesus' day, they recognize that God has come to them in the person of Jesus (verse 44).

Palm Sunday was a day of celebration, but the motivation of those who shouted praises was mixed and shallow. Many probably saw this as the beginning of a revolution; others were there for the show and loved seeing the miracles (verse 37). The real test of discipleship would come when the crowd turned. Would the true disciples stick with him? Some of us come from countries or cultures where we have enjoyed a degree of privilege as Christians. But will we stick with Jesus, even when the culture turns? Will we still be witnesses to the gospel when it means we will be misrepresented as fools, or worse, as dangerous, intolerant and even oppressive?

A student story

Thomas oversees a number of student groups in Austria. He remembers when the students on one campus decided to become more visible on campus and put up a stall in the main university square along with other clubs and societies. They expected most people to be polite but uninterested. But they were wrong on both counts! As they discovered later, a number of students were very interested in talking about the gospel, but first they had to endure a very unexpected and angry verbal assault from a group of students who opposed their right to be there and who tried to 'occupy' their space and prevent them from setting up. A few years ago perhaps these Christians would have been seen as a little eccentric, but harmless. Now, however, in our radically changing Western culture, they were regarded as dangerous and hateful. To be perceived in this negative light was quite traumatic for the students, but they persevered and God was with them. In spite of outright hostility, the young Christians were encouraged in their faith as friends started to respond to the message of Jesus.

It is great news for all of us that, despite our fickleness, the heart of Jesus which went out to Jerusalem that day goes out to us today with the same depth of love. Neither our blindness nor our unfaithfulness can stop him from loving us or weeping over us. The disciples, and Peter in particular, would learn this over the next few days.

PRAY:

Lord Jesus, you know my heart. Just as you knew that your closest friends would be fickle and deny you, so you know that I am just as likely to do the same. With your Spirit's help, make me steadfast in my love and loyalty to you, the living, conquering King. When my eyes make me question who is winning the battle, keep my heart turned towards you, my lips praising your name and my words giving glory to the one who has won the victory. Amen.

THE WIDER STORY

READ: LUKE 20:1 – 22:38

This is a period of intensifying conflict between Jesus and the religious authorities, and several times we read of them trying to catch Jesus out (20:26), arrest him (20:19), or even kill him (19:47). Jesus has just cleared out the Temple and rebuked those who were making money out of worship (19:45–46). Chapter 20 is then characterized by a series of trick questions on issues of theology and politics (verses 2, 21, 27), which Jesus often answers with questions of his own (verses 4, 24, 41), until they don't dare ask him any more (verse 40). In between, he tells 'the parable of the tenants' as a picture of his own impending rejection and death (20:9–19) as well as a rebuke to the religious leaders of the day for being content in their own self-righteousness and refusing to repent. Chapter 20:45–47 is also a stinging criticism of those who delight in status but 'devour widows' while it is a widow who demonstrates true faith and generosity to God (21:1–4).

The rest of Chapter 21 is an extended sermon on the signs of the end times, beginning with the destruction of Jerusalem (verses 20–21; see also verse 6) and ending with the second coming (verses 27–28). But it is not a chronological timetable. Many of these signs (verses 9–11) are visible in every generation and serve as reminders to 'watch out' (verse 8). Chapter 22:1–38 records Judas' plot to betray Jesus and Jesus' last meal with his disciples.

REFLECT:

- Consider Jesus' response to the trick questions in Chapter 20. What can we learn from his example about how to deal wisely with those who use political or theoretical objections to avoid taking his claims seriously?

- How can the 'signs of the end' mentioned in Chapter 21 keep us alert and missionally motivated, without being distracted by pointless speculation?
- Look at the conversation in 22:14–38. What do you learn about Jesus? Or about the disciples? Pray that your faith will not fail and that you will be able to strengthen others (verse 32).

AN EVENING PSALM

READ: PSALM 118

You will recognize verses 26–27 from this morning's reading (see also John 12:13). You can imagine a crowd chanting it (a little like at a sports match): verses 1–7 are a 'call and response' and the main section of the psalm (verses 8–21) is confident and triumphant. Look at the number of references to victory, joy and salvation from death. The singers know that only the righteous can enter into the presence of the Lord (verses 19–21); they know that it is God, not human rulers, who should be trusted, and that he alone brings victory (verses 8, 9, 16). But it is a victory that comes from being rejected by those who saw themselves as 'the builders' (verse 22). In fact, Jesus quotes verse 22 in the next chapter (see Luke 20:17). Yes, we can sing this psalm with true joy and confidence, but only because of what was achieved by the rejected one who defeated death finally and decisively (verses 17–18). Read this psalm in the light of the gospel story and what happens after Jesus rides into Jerusalem. Give thanks, remembering that the psalm begins and ends with the everlasting love of God (verses 1–4, 29).

'I DON'T KNOW HIM'

READ: LUKE 22:39–62

> *Then Peter remembered the word the Lord had spoken to him: 'Before the cock crows today, you will disown me three times.'*
>
> LUKE 22:61

Betrayal is one of the most painful things any of us can endure. It cuts deeper than many physical injuries, its effects last longer than many diseases. It forces us to question our own judgment and makes us feel that it is impossible for us to trust in the same way again. Injury caused to us by a stranger or an acquaintance can be difficult, but betrayal usually comes from a close friend, a family member or a spouse. It is devastating. Jesus himself is about to experience that betrayal at the hands of his friends, and from two in particular. Here we will see, in yet deeper ways, how he empathizes with us in all of our weaknesses (Hebrews 4:15) and truly '[bears] our griefs and [carries] our sorrows' (Isaiah 53:4, NKJV).

Earlier we learned how the disciples' weaknesses are not hidden from us in the Gospels: they can be crass, arrogant, prejudiced and often very slow to understand what Jesus is saying. As we approach the final days of Jesus' life, one thing can be certain: if he was relying on his disciples to protect him or fight for him, he was going to be bitterly disappointed. In these verses we see them falling asleep, losing their temper and running away until finally the so-called ringleader actually denies ever knowing him.

Falling into temptation

Twice, Jesus encourages his disciples to pray so that they will not 'fall into temptation' (verses 40, 46). He doesn't specify what the temptation might be, but it is certainly an encouragement to pray. Because this is what Jesus himself does, so earnestly that his emotional turmoil results in the physical manifestation of bleeding. Compared to his earnest, heartbreaking prayers, the disciples didn't last a few minutes before they fell asleep. Luke emphasizes the sharp contrast between Jesus relying on divine strength (verse 43) and the disciples in their human frailty (verse 45). Of course they were exhausted, scared and sad, but Jesus had pointed them towards the only remedy for such fatigue and fear: prayer. When the disciples were scared, they slept; when Jesus was faced with betrayal and death, he prayed.

The temptation to fight

Once they had woken, the disciples responded to the crisis in two opposite ways, both of them wrong. Firstly, in the face of the treachery of one of their own, there was a brief moment of bravado. They offered to defend Jesus with swords and one of them (we know it was Peter – see John 18:10) got as far as injuring a servant. As resistance goes, it was quite pathetic and short-lived. Jesus puts a stop to it and heals the servant. He doesn't want or need to be defended by human weapons. When faced by betrayal or suffering personal injury of some sort, there will always be the temptation for us to fight back. Sometimes we may even feel we are fighting to defend Jesus. We must take care not to fall into temptation and respond in ungodly ways in our actions, words – or even our computer keyboards. We must not become warriors that require Jesus' rebuke.

The temptation to run

Secondly, if they weren't allowed to fight, then the disciples thought there was only one alternative: to run (see Matthew 26:56; Mark 14:50). For Peter, after his abortive episode with the sword, his defection began with him keeping his distance (verse 54) and then led to outright denial that he even knew who this Jesus was (verses 56–60). However, there was another alternative the disciples could have taken; neither fighting with human weapons, nor running and denying, but standing and fighting the forces of darkness with the spiritual weapons of love and truth. They could have remained by Jesus' side even if it resulted in the same fate. They could have loved their master by following him the whole way. They could have overcome their enemies by forgiving them. Instead, they ran and disowned him. You see, the irony is that what Peter said was true. He didn't really know Jesus at all.

We know that, probably, we would have fared no better. So often we fight when we should run, or at least stand; and we run when we should stand and fight. It doesn't disqualify us from discipleship or put us beyond God's grace, but it should make us humble and prayerful. Above all, as we see how Jesus dealt with betrayal, we should have no doubt that he is able to feel and to heal any of those scars that we still bear.

Of course, this sad and shameful episode needs to be seen in the context of the whole story. Jesus' arrest and death was something he endured voluntarily; and Peter's treatment of Jesus did not diminish Jesus' love for him. After his resurrection, Jesus still counted Peter as one of his disciples, even if Peter no longer regarded himself as one (Mark 16:7). And at a beach barbecue a few days later, Peter would be restored and recommissioned to a new ministry which he would engage in with renewed courage and deeper devotion (see John 21:15 and the following verses).

PRAY:

> *Lord Jesus, my experience of betrayal might be as small as a childhood friend sharing my secret, or as huge as a spouse having an affair, but you know and can feel my pain because you were utterly abandoned by your closest friends. Thank you that you can identify with me in my betrayals. When it comes to identifying with you, give me the courage, not to be tempted to fight or flee, but to stand firm. Help me not to fear or follow anything that takes me away from you. In your victorious name I pray, Amen.*

THE WIDER STORY

READ: LUKE 22:63 – 23:12

Between Jesus' arrest and his crucifixion we have the various 'mock trials' of Jesus. These are essentially 'mistrials' not just by modern expectations, but even by the standards of both Roman and Jewish law at that time. We see Jesus suffer injustice at the hands of the guards (verses 63–65), the chief priests and Jewish elders (verses 66–71), the Roman governor Pilate (23:1–6, 13–25) and the Judean king, Herod (verses 7–12). Neither Pilate nor Herod wanted to take responsibility for Jesus' fate, passing the buck to each other until Pilate makes a final offer to release a prisoner – hoping that this would get him 'off the hook'. It didn't work!

REFLECT:

- What does this section teach us about earthly power and justice? How is the impending crucifixion of Jesus going to address those issues once and for all?
- How can these final days of Jesus' life help us respond when we experience betrayal or injustice?

AN EVENING PSALM

READ: PSALM 55

This is a cry for help from someone in trouble (verses 1–5). When we are in anguish the natural feeling is to escape to a safe or 'happy place' (verses 6–8). But this is not a final solution. We need the evil and violence to be dealt with (verses 9–11, 15). The picture of the destructive forces at work (verse 11) reminds us of the hatred in Jerusalem as Jesus approached his last days and of course verses 12–14 are poignant when we think of how his best friends betrayed him. But the psalm finishes with a note of faith and hope. It is framed by the words 'as for me' (verses 16, 23). *Even though* there is evil and violence, treachery and betrayal, the psalmist will still stand apart and trust the Lord. Whatever trials we have to face, we can be assured that because of Jesus – who was abandoned, betrayed and not spared the 'terrors of death' (verse 4) – evil will not ultimately triumph. Make the last sentence of this psalm your statement of faith tonight and hold on to the promise of verse 22.

DYING WELL

READ: LUKE 23:26–56

> *Jesus said, 'Father, forgive them, for they do not know what they are doing.'*
>
> LUKE 23:34

Crowds can be dangerous. People do things in crowds they would not do on their own. Positively, popular demonstrations have brought about needed change in many countries, but crowds can also be prone to easy manipulation and a 'mob mentality'. I remember, at a time of great political tension in my own country, how a peace negotiation had just been signed by the opposing sides – but of course it was not accepted by everyone.

Ironically, it happened on Good Friday and my church happened to be beside the parliament buildings. After our evening service and reflection on this passage, I strolled up to the parliament building where a mob had gathered to shout insults and berate the politicians who had signed the treaty. They were trying to break down the gates and hit passing cars. I got a new perspective on how quickly 'normal people' could be whipped up by a few. The events of the first 'Good Friday' demonstrate this dynamic most powerfully. We saw two days ago how the crowd welcomed Jesus. Now there is an about turn as many of them approve of his execution.

This is the day when an innocent man was killed and a guilty man went free; this is the day when the sun was darkened and the earth shook; this is the day when God himself took the assault of hell so that we could experience the embrace of heaven. This is one of the most powerful crowd scenes in the Gospels, but any good movie director would balance the chaos and agitation of the surging multitude by focusing in on the individuals who, for just a moment, take the spotlight.

Perhaps we have known people who were friends but then disappeared from our lives once we faced difficulty, illness or trials. It is significant that all of these men saw Jesus at his lowest point of humiliation, and at a time when all his long-standing companions had deserted him. Yet it was in the weakness and shame of Good Friday, not in the pomp and power of Palm Sunday, that many of these men were attracted to him. Let's consider the different individuals in the scene.

The condemned (Luke 23:18–25)

It is interesting that the sort of trouble Jesus stirs up is regarded as more dangerous and threatening to the establishment than that caused by a rabble-rousing criminal. Barabbas was in the condemned cell awaiting execution for insurrection and murder. But still the people – and Pilate – thought it safer to have him back on the streets than Jesus. As the one who was released because Jesus was going to die in his place, Barabbas stands as a type, a representative of all believers. We were rebels and deserving of death until Christ stepped in and chose death so that we might live (see Romans 5:10).

The cross-carrier (Luke 23:26)

Simon was probably no more than a casual bystander, a visitor who was in the wrong place at the wrong time and found himself taking the role of an extra in this grotesque drama. It was unusual for a condemned man not to carry his own cross, but this reminds us of the toll that the whipping and beatings had taken on Jesus' body (see Matthew 27:26–31). As he stumbled under the weight of the cross, publicly humiliated and unable to complete this final journey on his own, it shows us the extent of his physical suffering. Simon and his family were probably disciples known to the early church (compare Mark 15:21; Romans 16:13) and he becomes a metaphor for all disciples who, in obedience to Jesus' instructions, 'take up their cross and follow [him]' (Luke 9:23–24). Normally, someone would only carry a cross if they are going to end up *on it*. In following Jesus, we die to our own desires and ambitions.

The convicted criminal (Luke 23:39–43)

We also get a fascinating insight into the psyche of two men who find themselves facing certain death. One is consumed by his own bitterness, even blaming Jesus for not getting them out of this situation. The other has an acute sense of his own guilt but also of Jesus' innocence and, what's more, an inkling that this dying man beside him may indeed still have the power to welcome him into paradise. When faced with our own mortality we can either 'rage against the dying of the light'[2] or find a deep faith and deeper peace in the one who on this Good Friday defeated death itself for us.

The convinced centurion (Luke 23:47)

As Jesus breathed his last, a battle-hardened Roman centurion for whom this barbaric spectacle was just

2 Dylan Thomas, 'Do not go gentle into that good night' in *The Collected Poems of Dylan Thomas: The Original Edition* (New Directions, 2010), p148.

another familiar day's work, recognized that there was something unique occurring here. Perhaps an accumulation of the darkness and earthquake (which caused the Temple curtain to be torn – see Matthew 27:51) and also the demeanour and words of Jesus as he died, caused this hardened soldier to stop and recognize who this was. Different Gospel writers and different translations record the centurion's words in various ways. It could mean simply 'This man was innocent' (Luke 23:47, ESV), 'a righteous man' (Luke 23:47, NIV), or 'the Son of God' (Matthew 27:54). While this was not what we would understand as a Christian confession of Jesus' deity, it was still a powerful eyewitness testimony from someone whose only encounter with Jesus was watching how he died. Similarly, Christians who die well can win many for Christ.

The grave-giver (Luke 23:50–53)

The fifth cameo in this story is of a man who was once counted among the enemies of Jesus but who had come to believe and who was prepared to sacrifice his reputation and even his family's burial plot for this man he had only observed for a few years. He is also a metaphor for all disciples who, once enemies, are now family and who find their ultimate resting place in him.

The Arimathean

*Now there was a man named Joseph ... who had
not consented to their decision ... He came from the
Judean town of Arimathea, and ... was waiting for
the kingdom of God.*

LUKE 23:50–51

Waiting
for the kingdom of God:
not nailed-down verdicts,
or trumped-up charges,
nor law and justice
bent.
He did not consent.

Waiting
for his moment to stand:
to nail his colours,
to take his side.
The final curtain –
the end –
turned sceptic friend.

Waiting
for permission to go
and remove the nails,
and dress the wounds,
and give his last gift.
A tomb –
or a waiting room?

DAITHI MACIOMAIRE

PRAY:

Jesus, help me not to fall under the influence of a crowd, the wrong crowd, the invisible online 'crowd'. As I see the way ordinary people were drawn into this story, I rejoice again in the way you also drew me in. Like Barabbas, I have been set free because you refused to walk free; I have been made alive because you chose to die. The description of your suffering is painful for me to behold even 2,000 years later, but like the thief on the cross, you hold out words of promise to me. You have the words of eternal life. Even in your deepest pain your love for others and for me is uppermost. Thank you for the depth of your love. Amen.

THE WIDER STORY

READ: LUKE 23:13–25

This is the climax of the 'trial' when the people choose a political prisoner, Barabbas, to be released instead of Jesus and, not having the courage of his convictions, Pilate hands Jesus over to be crucified. It was a political decision taken out of cowardice to prevent public disorder.

REFLECT:

- Jesus could have called the army of heaven to deliver him (see Matthew 26:53) but rather chose to bear human injustice. Reflect on why he did this.
- What insights have these chapters given you about the cross and its necessity for our salvation?

AN EVENING PSALM

READ: PSALM 88

This is the darkest psalm in the Bible. It is honest and transparent. It contains no easy answers and no rays of light (well, almost none). While many laments will finish with a note of hope, this one ends with 'darkness is my closest friend' (verse 18). Although we are not explicitly told, this psalm could have been in the mind of Jesus as he approached the cross. The psalmist is near to death (verses 3–5); he is 'in the pit' (verses 6–7); he is totally alone (verses 8–9); he is frightened and despairing and cannot remember a time when it was any different (verses 15–17). These are all characteristics of depression, and the fact that the Bible contains the words and prayers of someone in that situation reminds us that it is not a sin to feel like this. But we also see that his depression is not totally self-focused. He is perplexed because his current situation does not bring glory to God (verses 10–14) and most importantly of all, although he is fearful and at his wit's end, he is still talking to the God who seems so far away. He is directing his complaint upwards, not inwards (verses 1–2, 9, 13); God is still the God of his salvation (verse 1). If this is your prayer today, be encouraged that other good men and women have been there before you, and hold on to verses 1 and 2, remembering that the one you are praying to has also been there to ensure that there will always be a way out of the darkness.

A NEW DAY

READ: LUKE 24:1–35

> *Why do you look for the living among the dead?*
> *He is not here; he has risen!*
>
> LUKE 24:5–6

One of the most effective student evangelists in the English-speaking world was the late Michael Green who conducted university missions over a period of six decades. The night before he died he rang a good friend and, full of his usual *joie de vivre*, he said 'I'm ready to go. I've looked again this evening at the evidence for the resurrection, and I know it's true, I'm ready to go!' The resurrection of Jesus Christ is the foundation of Christianity; without it the whole edifice crumbles. We will look at this more tomorrow. But in this simple narrative Luke captures the unexpected nature of what was happening. The women were 'perplexed' (verse 4, ESV); the men thought it was all fiction (verse 11). There is no logical basis to any scenario that suggests the disciples made up the story or stole the body themselves. The episodes in Luke 24 show us that the disciples were unbelieving, mystified and grieving (verses 11, 12, 17). The first witnesses were women, whose testimony was invalid in court at this time.

But then suddenly, little by little, individuals, small groups and large groups begin to encounter the risen Christ in diverse places and in everyday circumstances that could not be interpreted or dismissed as mere hallucinations. The closed worldview of these first-century Jews was shattered as they tried to make sense of this.

Grief that obscures the reality of Jesus

In our grief we often can't recognize Jesus walking with us. The first appearance recorded by Luke is of two brokenhearted disciples walking away from Jerusalem completely disillusioned. This pair, possibly a man and wife (why have artists always presumed it was two men?), had pinned their hopes on Jesus and now feel abandoned and let down by God. When Jesus starts to walk with them, they treat him as a stranger – perhaps they were saying to themselves, *'It can't be Jesus; he's dead!'* Even though they now had his physical presence as evidence on top of the women's testimony (verses 22–24), they weren't ready to believe.

Grief that requires the comforting presence and words of Jesus

As the disciples open up about their shattered hopes and their despair, Jesus could have stopped them and said 'Look! Look! It's me!' He could have done what he did to Thomas and told them to put their hands in the nail prints (see John 20). But he deals with us all individually in our grief or doubt. What was right for Thomas was not right for this pair. So, for them, he gives them a Bible overview lesson (verses 25–27). Why? Perhaps because he knew what was needed by these disciples (whom we don't hear of again). Maybe they required different proofs to Thomas, so that after Jesus had ascended and the appearances stopped and when the doubts came, they didn't just have a faint memory of a bizarre encounter on the country road. No, they could look back to all the scriptures of the Old Testament and reassure each other that this was true. Jesus walked with them in person that day but would continue to walk with them each day as his Holy Spirit applied the Scriptures to their lives.

Grief that turns to joy

We don't know why the disciples' eyes were opened to Jesus' identity through the simple act of breaking bread (verses 31, 35). Maybe that is when they noticed the nail prints. Maybe there was something unique about the way Jesus broke bread that they recognized from spending time with him over the years – the way we can know someone by the unconscious little gestures they make. Whatever it was, as Jesus the guest unexpectedly took on the role of the host (verse 30), their eyes were opened. The despairing, tired disciples were so transformed by this experience that, ignoring their exhaustion and the darkness (verse 29), they ran the seven miles back to share the good news. The certainty and victory of the resurrection of Jesus dispels all darkness.

The breaking of the bread

We stood along the Galilean shore,
We heard some words we never heard before;
We tasted life, we saw five thousand fed,
We knew him in the breaking of the bread.
> And then one night they told us he had died,
> With nails and wood our dreams were crucified.

We talked about the things that we had seen,
We thought about the things that might have been;
Our heads were down, our hearts were far away,

When the stranger came and walked with us that day.
    He opened up the truths of ancient days,
    He gave us hope, he set our hearts ablaze.

We stopped him as he made to walk away,
We pleaded with him 'Step right in and stay';
But as we sat and pondered all he'd said,
We knew him in the breaking of the bread.
    Surprised by joy, we ran into the night,
    The streets were bathed in resurrection light.

And so we have a hope that never dies,
We know the one in whom our future lies,
And when the feast's prepared, the table spread,
We'll know him in the breaking of the bread.

DAITHI MACIOMAIRE

PRAY:

Resurrection Day! I praise you God, giver of life, that you had a plan beyond my imagining! Thank you that this day gives me a fresh start and a glorious hope like nothing else could ever do. I pray that with each new day, you would protect me from disillusionment and anything which would obscure your presence with me. May the joy and truth of your resurrection power inspire me to love, serve and worship. He is risen indeed – Hallelujah!

THE WIDER STORY

READ: LUKE 24:36–53

After this story, Luke 24:36–49 tells of Jesus appearing to the wider group as the Emmaus disciples were telling their story. There he proved the physicality of his resurrection by eating and, as he had done on the road earlier, 'open[ing] their minds so they could understand the Scriptures' (verse 45) – so that in days to come, should they ever question whether they had perhaps imagined all of this, they could look back and *know* that this had been foretold in their own Scriptures (verses 46–47). This Gospel account ends with the ascension of Jesus which is where Acts, Luke's second volume, begins and where he gives us a little more detail about what happened (compare Luke 24:50–53; Acts 1:1–8).

REFLECT:

- How do these verses add to the various pieces of evidence for the resurrection and help affirm your faith and hope?
- What have been the highlights for you as you have read the Gospel of Luke? How has it helped you know and understand Jesus better?

AN EVENING PSALM

READ: PSALM 24

This is a triumphant psalm, suitable for a day when we have been reading about the resurrection of Jesus. It tells of God's ownership of all creation (verses 1–2), of his holiness (verses 3–4) and that he is a God who blesses those who trust in him (verses 5–6). The repeated chorus (verses 7–10) is a 'call and response' and the image is of a crowd standing at the city gates to welcome a triumphant king back from the battlefield. When Jesus rose from the dead he was victorious in the greatest cosmic battle of all time; sin and death were defeated and we can now, through him, have 'clean hands and a pure heart' (verse 4). Likewise, when he ascended to heaven, the gates would be opened for him and the angels would be singing as he took his rightful place on the throne (see Hebrews 4:14–16). Give thanks this evening for Jesus' victory.

PART 2: ACTS

GO!

READ: ACTS 1:1–11

> *But you will receive power when the Holy Spirit comes on you; and you will be my witnesses in Jerusalem, and in all Judea and Samaria, and to the ends of the earth.*
>
> ACTS 1:8

So many movie sequels never live up to the original. This is different! Luke's second book about Jesus will not disappoint us. We will be missing something important if we think his first book is about Jesus, and his second is about us, the church. No, Luke's Gospel was about *all that Jesus began to do and to teach* (verse 1) and now Luke sets us up for the sequel: *what he will continue to do*, by the Holy Spirit, through his church. Luke shows us from the very beginning four things that should characterize every church and every disciple.

Encounter – the church lives in the light of the resurrection

All Christian mission happens because of an encounter with the risen Jesus. In 2022 Gwen and I had the privilege of attending the Oberammergau Passion Play in Bavaria. It only takes place every ten years and is a phenomenal undertaking involving a cast and crew of hundreds. It was an unforgettable, clear presentation of the teachings of Jesus and the events leading to his death, powerfully portrayed. However, although the play did end with an empty tomb, the bodily resurrection of Jesus was disappointingly absent. There was a sense of mystery at the end which is in sharp contrast to Luke's testimony that Jesus left 'convincing proofs' (verse 3) of his resurrection, and that it was this encounter with their risen Lord that transformed the disciples. They could not have built a church or endured decades of persecution based on mystery or uncertainty. Nothing that happened from now on in the New Testament could have happened had it not been for the living Lord Jesus.

Empowerment – the church lives by the power of the Holy Spirit

For the disciples, to try to found a global church (verse 8) in their own strength would have been like an army going into battle without protection and with misfiring weapons. Jesus doesn't send his people into spiritual battle with faulty equipment. That's why he told his disciples to wait for the Spirit. The resurrection appearances were spectacular proof, but now, no longer limited to time, space or geography, the resurrected, living Lord Jesus is active in his church through his Holy Spirit: convicting people of their need of Jesus, drawing them to Jesus and empowering them to live their newborn resurrection lives.

I'm sure most of us know what it is like to lose someone special to us. The disciples would have felt bereft. But the coming of the Spirit was not a cheap second best. It wasn't like when you go to the theatre to watch a world-famous actress, only to find out she is ill and it is her understudy instead. No, the coming of the Spirit was the coming of God himself in the third person of the Trinity.

Envisioning – the church lives with a global perspective

Why was the Spirit given? Not primarily to enhance our own personal devotional life, but so that the world could be reached with this life-changing message. So Jesus opens his followers' eyes to the bigger picture.

How would they do it, this fearful, uneducated bunch who didn't have a great track record in lasting the race? How were they going to achieve the mission of being the witnesses in Jerusalem, Judea, Samaria and the ends of the earth (verse 8)? Jerusalem, where the enemies of Jesus were still searching for his followers; Judea, their homeland where they would be open to ridicule; Samaria, their cultural and political enemy with centuries of mutual hatred; the ends of the earth, given that they were twelve unschooled young men with no independent income in the days before budget airlines! That was the seemingly impossible vision.

And it is a vision we still have. I am privileged to work with an organization founded on a similar global vision: that is, to have 'an evangelical student witness in every university in the world'. In one of our gatherings I heard a worship song in Greenlandic, sung by a couple working in Nuuk and accompanied by a guitarist from Punta Arenas in southernmost Chile. We have students reaching other students with this gospel message from Fairbanks, Alaska, to Dunedin, southern New Zealand. The task of Acts 1:8 is well underway but there will always be so much still to do. That is why the first words the disciples heard after Jesus left were words of encouragement.

Expectation – the church lives with its eyes on the return of Jesus

In verses 10–11 Jesus has gone and the disciples are left staring upwards. They are told not to be afraid because he is coming back. I believe the church faces two opposite temptations in our mission and discipleship. There is the temptation to be idle or introspective and stand as it were, 'staring into heaven' waiting for his return, forgetting the command of verse 8 'to go'. The other temptation is activism where we forget that verse 8 is a prophecy of who we will be (his witnesses) and not what we will do – so sometimes we forget it is *his* mission, not ours. Reaching the world should not replace sensitivity to his leading; nor should our strategies replace true spiritual dependence.

By the time we reach verse 11, Jesus has gone – and yet he hasn't! As verse 1 reminded us, he *continues* to work by his Spirit through his church, because he has ascended. The ascension does not end with Jesus suspended in the clouds. The rest of the New Testament makes clear that having ascended, Jesus sat down at God's right hand to exercise authority over all earthly powers (see Ephesians 1:20; Hebrews 1:3; 8:1; 12:2). We live out the inspiring vision of verse 8 in the knowledge that the risen and ascended Jesus is still leading and protecting his church through history.

PRAY:

Dear Lord, thank you for your Word. Today we see the thrust of the gospel into all the world, from our doorsteps to unknown cities and towns. Make us mindful today of all your servants. For some it has involved a calling and commitment to travel to another part of the world and proclaim your

Word with power. For others it will be staying and witnessing in their own family, workplace and neighbourhood; they too are proclaiming your Word with power. Wherever we may find ourselves today, give us power to see your kingdom extended and your name glorified. In Jesus' name we pray, Amen.

LORNA MOORE – IFES EUROPE REGIONAL TEAM

THE WIDER STORY

READ: ACTS 1:12–26

The second part of the chapter fills out the time between Jesus' ascension and Pentecost (Acts 2) and includes a sad postscript to the Judas story (verses 18–20). The disciples (120 of them) appear to have spent these weeks in prayer and reflection on the Scriptures. They then chose Matthias to take Judas' place. Notice the requirements for an apostle: someone who had been with Jesus throughout his ministry and was a witness to the resurrection (verses 21–22).

REFLECT:

- Look again at how the disciples spent their 'waiting time'. How easy do we find it to wait for the Lord's guidance?
- The disciples prayed and then 'cast lots' (verse 26). As we look ahead to what happens in Chapter 2, why do you think we never read again of casting lots as a method of Christian guidance?

AN EVENING PSALM

READ: PSALM 47

This psalm pictures God as a conquering king going up to sit on his throne over the nations (verse 5). In the light of this morning's reading we can view this with even greater clarity. At the end of his earthly ministry Jesus ascended and empowered his church to spread the news to all nations that he is their rightful king. Almost every verse of this psalm mentions the nations. He is their king and they are called to praise him. A fellowship such as IFES, with groups in over 170 countries, is in a unique position to understand the truth and wonder of this psalm. Every time we meet internationally, we experience something of what the psalmist calls us to. Think of the friendships you have across the nations and praise God that all kings and nations belong to him. Whether those countries are at peace or war, experiencing poverty or wealth; whether their rulers are corrupt or have integrity – they are ultimately in his hands and will be answerable to his judgment. However, verse 9 presents us with the vision of many rulers being incorporated into God's people. While ultimately God will exercise judgment on unrepentant oppressors and tyrants, his desire is that they and their people come to know him and experience the joy of his family. In this day of media saturation, it's likely we know more presidents and prime ministers than ever before, so pray for those who God places on your heart. And sing praise to the King of kings (verse 6).

A NEW POWER

READ: ACTS 2:1–47

All of them were filled with the Holy Spirit and began to speak in other tongues as the Spirit enabled them.

ACTS 2:4

I've never been a massive music festival-goer. Sleeping in a tent on hard ground and not showering for five days while your neighbours get progressively more drunk and the Irish weather gets increasingly wet was never my idea of fun. Maybe it would have been different had I lived in a warmer climate – although I imagine the noise and the crowds and the smells may still have been too much for me.

The religious life of the Jewish people centred around festivals; sometimes they even involved camping (Leviticus 23:42–43). But what took place at this festival bore no resemblance to anything that had happened before at such a gathering. By the end of the day over 3,000 people's lives would be irrevocably changed; they would start on a journey that for many of them would lead to both a better life and an untimely death. For the men who were at the centre of it, the day had not quite turned out how they expected either. So much had happened in their lives recently that they weren't much in the mood for entering in to the spirit of the festival.

In fact, they were gathered indoors somewhere (probably the room that had been acting as their base for the past seven weeks) simply waiting. They were shut off from the gathering momentum outside. They had no expectation whatsoever that by the end of the day they would be thrust into the limelight in one of the most amazing events ever witnessed in Jerusalem. Yet within a few hours these men were utterly transformed. Seven weeks ago the main spokesman Peter couldn't even admit to a servant girl who he was. Now, changed by truth itself, he speaks boldly and convincingly right into people's hearts, and 3,000 believe!

What had happened? We may be fascinated by the spectacular phenomenon: the wind (power); the fire (purity); the tongues (in this case, human languages enabling all visitors to Jerusalem to hear the gospel instantaneously) but the chapter is more concerned with the message itself and the effect it had on the hearers (verses 37–41).

Without the Holy Spirit we cannot communicate

People heard and believed! There was obviously a miracle at work in the ears and hearts of the audience, but there was also a miracle at work in the disciples. Jesus had told them to wait until the Spirit came because he knew the task was beyond mere human endeavour, gifting or cleverness – even if they were exceptionally talented, which they weren't.

Two things would have prevented the disciples being able to stand up publicly and speak so effectively, and they are the two things which might prevent us from doing the same thing: 'won't' and 'can't'. Either we lack the courage or we lack the resources. But the Holy Spirit gives us the courage to witness and the resources for the mission to which God calls us.

Without the Holy Spirit we cannot change

That day, 3,000 people suddenly saw the light. But while everyone was amazed (verse 7) and some were deeply moved (verse 37), others mocked (verse 13). It's one thing to have the light go on, but if all that means is that we have more head knowledge, or we try just that little bit harder to keep God's Law, then the death of Christ and the coming of the Spirit would all be in vain. However, this is something different. The response to Peter's message is that they 'were cut to the heart' and asked Peter what they should do (verse 37). His answer was simple: Repent! Stop and turn around. Be baptized! Humble yourselves and become part of a new family. At this time baptism was something that mainly happened to Gentiles who converted to Judaism. Practising Jews would not see their need of it (although John the Baptist had prepared the way with his preaching of repentance, see Luke 3:3). The Holy Spirit works in those who are humbly willing to demonstrate their own weakness and dependence.

Without the Holy Spirit Christian communities cannot function

The end of Chapter 2 describes a radically changed community; one that could only be sustained by God himself. The disciples, with their history of in-fighting, bickering and backstabbing (compare Luke 9:46, 49, 54; Mark 10:37; John 21:20–22), certainly couldn't live like this without help. But we see here how the church emerges out of this context of supernaturally transformed lives. It is a church which was birthed by the Holy Spirit and sustained by the Holy Spirit. John Stott reminds us that 'as a body without breath is a corpse, so the church without the Spirit is dead.'[3]

3 John Stott, *The Message of Acts* (InterVarsity Press, 2014), p27.

When I started as an undergraduate, I found out that the Christian group on campus was basically starting from scratch again. The previous year it had torn itself apart in internal wranglings about the Holy Spirit and charismatic gifts. There had been no effective evangelistic outreach for two years, and it took four years for the group to regain its strength and visibility on campus. What a tragedy! What really would have pleased the Holy Spirit would have been to see unity and vision for gospel outreach.

A student story

In contrast, a few years ago at a regional conference in Fiji, the various student movements from around the Pacific stood with their flags and asked for prayer for the ministries and events they had coming up in the months ahead. There were three international students from the Solomon Islands present. There was at that time no similar student group on the islands. They hadn't even got a flag of their country with them, but they had been challenged by what they had heard and seen. They made a small flag, walked to the front and asked for prayer that, by the power of the Holy Spirit, one day there would be groups like this in the Solomon Islands. It all looked quite weak and pathetic. But God uses the weak things of this world to confound the wise and, encouraged by what they had learned at that regional conference, they returned to their homeland. Within a couple of years, because of the vision of those few students, a new student movement was planted in the Solomon Islands.

The important thing when it comes to the Holy Spirit is to remember that he never draws attention to himself. He continues the ministry of Jesus. He is the Holy Spirit of Jesus; he always points to Jesus. It is Jesus whom most of this chapter is about and it is his Holy Spirit who will come alongside us and enable us to be the people we were called to be. So thank the Lord Jesus that he has given us his very Spirit so that he can still walk this earth, speak, open eyes, change lives and build little communities of faith through us.

PRAY:

> *Thank you, Lord Jesus, for the amazing gift of your Spirit. Make us draw near to you and be filled again and again with the Holy Spirit. Work in us and through us so we will have the courage to witness to the people that you place on our paths. Thank you that you want to give us every spiritual gift we need for the mission you are calling us to do in our lives. Show us our own weakness and dependence on you in everything we do. Help us to repent and change anything that is not according to your will. Let us be like the early church so our communities will draw others in and to yourself so that your name will be glorified and praised. In your name we pray, Amen.*

FRANCINA DE PATER – IFES EUROPE ASSOCIATE REGIONAL SECRETARY

THE WIDER STORY

READ: ACTS 3:1–26

This chapter tells the story of the miraculous healing of a man lame from birth (verses 1–10) and then Peter's powerful sermon to the crowd who had witnessed it (verses 11–26). It is Jesus, not Peter or John, who has healed the man (verses 12, 16). The sermon focuses on the guilt of the people in handing Jesus over to be crucified only weeks before (verses 12–15) and the message that there is now an opportunity to repent, be forgiven and renewed, and enjoy the rule of the Messiah (verses 19–20) who has come in fulfilment of the Scriptures (verses 21–26).

REFLECT:

- What do we learn about Jesus from the names that Peter gives him in verses 13–15? What titles of Jesus might be most relevant to our audience as we witness?
- Verse 19 mentions repentance, forgiveness and refreshing. This is not a 'one-time process'. In what ways do you need that process today in your life and work?

AN EVENING PSALM

READ: PSALM 16

This evening we read the full psalm that Peter quoted on that momentous day in Jerusalem. The verses that Peter quoted (verses 8–11) tell of how the psalmist was secure – that God would indeed be his refuge, as he had prayed in verse 1. He was certain that God would deliver him from death. In the original context God did answer David's prayer on many occasions, rescuing him from Saul and from many subsequent enemies – not just Philistines and Amorites, but also those within his own family. However, the time came for David to die; he was not immortal. So Peter uses this psalm to preach the resurrection and hope of eternal life that can be ours through trusting in Christ, whose rising from the dead gives us the certain hope that we will not be abandoned to the grave or see decay (verse 10).

While we do pray that God would turn back our enemies and rescue us when we are oppressed, we know from Scripture and from the stories of those who are being martyred in every generation that sometimes he asks for his children to pay the ultimate sacrifice, and that all of us will one day see death. The good news is that that is never the end of the story for those who hope in Christ. Reflect on the 'pleasant places' (verse 6) where God has led you. Trust him that in any current difficulty you 'will not be shaken' (verse 8) and pray that even this evening you would know 'fullness of joy' in his presence (verse 11).

DAY 18

WE CAN'T KEEP IT TO OURSELVES

READ: ACTS 4:1–31

> *Which is right in God's eyes: to listen to you, or to him? You be the judges! As for us, we cannot help speaking about what we have seen and heard.*
>
> ACTS 4:19–20

When the Good News of Jesus is preached, people notice

Faith in Christ is intensely personal, but it is never private. There was nothing private about Jesus' ministry, and there was nothing private about the Holy Spirit's ministry through the apostles. People noticed – they couldn't help it. With powerful words and powerful deeds Peter preached and healed, demonstrating that God had come in Jesus Christ. The authorities couldn't put an end to Jesus two months previously, and they were now powerless to put an end to him by punishing the apostles. People were noticing: 5,000 of them (verse 4) – so many that the authorities dare not punish them (verse 21). Yet even these religious leaders noticed something significant: that they had been with Jesus (verse 13).

When the Good News of Jesus is preached, don't expect a rational response

One thing that stands out in the debates is that the opponents have no substance to their arguments.

Somehow, resurrection is bad news (verse 2); an act of kindness is bad news (verse 9). The arguments had nothing to do with truth or reality and everything to do with vested interests and personal and political agenda.

The opponents were a diverse group of Sadducees, priests and temple guards (verse 1). If the resurrection was true, the Sadducees were finished as a credible force (see Matthew 22:23). Annas and Caiaphas (verse 6) were involved in the arrest of Jesus (John 18:24), so if he was alive, the priests were finished as a moral authority. If what Jesus said about the Temple was true (Matthew 24:2) then the temple guards were finished as a civic influence. This unholy alliance had so much to lose economically, politically and spiritually, so they would try anything to stop the message spreading, regardless of its truth. While it is important to show the reasonable nature of the Christian faith, as we see elsewhere (eg Acts 17:17) we must remember that those who raise objections to the Christian faith will not be convinced by reason alone, because their objections are often more rooted in the heart than in the mind. They have too much to lose if the gospel is true.

We cannot keep this Good News to ourselves

The apostles asked the authorities: 'Who should we obey, God or humans?' Their opponents were teachers of the Old Testament Law so they knew the Scriptures, and that there was only one answer! Peter and John then finish their defence with this wonderful proof of how, when the gospel of Jesus really gets hold of you, you cannot keep it to yourself (verse 20).

A student story

A few years ago, some of my friends who work with students in quite a hostile environment were arrested by the authorities in their country for holding an evangelistic event and were in danger of being imprisoned. When the time came for them to give their defence in court, the leader of the student group asked for prayer. For what? That she might find an opportunity to give the judge a Bible! Of course this could have been seen as a bribe, so the judge declined. In the end, the judge decided on a compromise and the students were fined for so-called 'illegal activity'. But the fine was the smallest possible that the judge could set: just a few dollars. After the court case, the students sent another request for prayer to some of us. What did they ask for this time? Peace and safety? Justice for themselves? That they would be more cautious in the future? No! They asked for prayer for their meeting the following week when they would be planning even more evangelistic events. Like Peter and John, they had the privilege of bearing witness to Christ in court and, like them, after their ordeal was over, they still couldn't keep the Good News to themselves.

What have you experienced in your Christian life that means you just have to share it with others? Remember that this message is about hope, forgiveness and resurrection; it is about the only way of salvation (verse 12). If there had been any other way, Jesus would not have needed to have been born – much less died – so that we could know God. Such a message is made for sharing, no matter what opposition or threats we may face. Such a message leads to many transformed lives, and the formation of radical, transformed communities (verses 32–37).

PRAY:

> Lord, you are God, who made heaven and earth
> and the sea. You see that many universities try to
> exclude your message from the campus. Consider
> the threats and difficulties we are facing. We are
> joining in the prayer of the early church that you
> enable us 'to speak your word with great boldness'
> (Acts 4:29). Fill us with your Holy Spirit to speak,
> no matter what opposition or threats we may face.
> We pray that you may open doors at the places we
> are studying; give us opportunities so that our fellow
> students, our universities, our societies notice. Help
> us to share your wonderful message with clarity,
> creativity and sensitivity to our campus culture.
> 'Stretch out your hand to heal and perform signs
> and wonders through the name of your holy servant
> Jesus' (Acts 4:30). Amen.

CHRISTIAN PICHLER – IFES EUROPE ASSOCIATE
REGIONAL SECRETARY

THE WIDER STORY

READ: ACTS 4:32–37

The end of Chapter 4 mirrors the end of Chapter 2 with
another picture of the apostles living in total unity and
radical community (verses 32–35). Barnabas, who will
have a major part to play in the book, is introduced in
verse 36. His generosity and the mention of others selling
property and donating the proceeds (verses 34–37) prepare
us for the next story which we'll consider tomorrow.

REFLECT:

- What aspects of this early church life do you find most inspiring?
- What would you find most difficult about being part of such a community?
- Pray that the life of your Christian community would be characterized both by powerful testimony and powerful grace (verse 33).

AN EVENING PSALM

READ: PSALM 123

This is a psalm about the right type of submission. Peter and John were told to be submissive to the religious leaders who opposed and killed Jesus, but they replied that they had to submit to God rather than to human authorities. They could identify with this psalm of the pilgrims walking to Jerusalem with their eyes collectively fixed on their divine master and with a determination to worship him. Now, although Jerusalem was the place where they endured the contempt and ridicule of the arrogant (verses 3–4), they continued to fix their gaze on the same God who inspired these pilgrims and now would deliver them. The concept of submission is profoundly counter-cultural in today's world, but it is an essential quality of the disciple. Pray this evening that your heart would be submissive to God's will and your eyes fixed on him alone.

REALITY CHECK!

READ: ACTS 5:1–11

> *Then Peter said, 'Ananias, how is it that Satan has so filled your heart that you have lied to the Holy Spirit?'*
>
> ACTS 5:3

With only fifteen passages to choose out of the whole book of Acts, it would have been easy to avoid this difficult story of two people apparently being 'zapped' by God for what, at first glance, seems to be no more than a bit of financial irregularity. However, I have included it because it is important to know how to read bits of the Bible we *don't* want to believe, especially when they come in the middle of stories we *do* want to believe. All around this episode are great stories that many have taken as inspiration for their spiritual lives; the coming of the Holy Spirit in power, the healings, the account of this radical community who had all things in common (4:32–27) and the signs and wonders (5:12). But we don't know what to do with Ananias and Sapphira.

All of these early chapters remind us that we are dealing with a supernatural God who can intervene through his servants, to heal and restore lost lives. So it should not be a case of *can* he do this to Ananias and his wife, but *should* he? What sort of God is this who would cause two people to drop dead because of a minor offence and without any sort of fair trial? Or is that to misread what is happening here? I think it is. Let's start with what actually happened.

What was the crime?

Sin is more than a series of isolated actions. With each sin we can easily find ways of minimizing, justifying or explaining it away. However, sin is actually a deep-seated determination to keep control of our own lives. The actions are simply symptoms of this disease. With Ananias and Sapphira we get a window into their hearts. We are shown their character.

They were under no compulsion to sell. No one forced them; in Chapter 4 Barnabas and others did it voluntarily. Nor were they under any compulsion to give all the proceeds to the apostles. Peter tells them it was still at their disposal once it was sold (verse 4). They could have tithed it, or given 50% or 70%, but they decided to pretend they were giving it all – it would look better. Thirdly, they were under no compulsion to lie. When Peter confronted them, he was giving them a chance to own up. Instead, they chose to continue their charade and, rather than bear the shame, they chose to lie. At various stages we see an accumulation of guilt as they corrupt the church with their greed and with their determination to appear better than others by deception and lying.

Why did Ananias die and Peter survive?

Let's not forget it is Peter who is doing the confronting here – and he was no stranger to shame (see Day 13). Was denying Jesus not worse than fiddling the books? The fact is: Peter was as guilty of deception in lying to save his own skin as Ananias was in lying to hoard funds for himself. So why did Ananias die and Peter survive? Peter survived because his heart was still alive to God's grace; Ananias died because his heart was consistently closed to anything but his own self-interest. His death was not the result of this one isolated incident, but because it was the culmination of decades of life choices.

There is a similar story in the Old Testament (2 Samuel 6) when the ark of God was being played about with like some lucky charm and carelessly moved from place to place on a cattle cart. It was touched by Uzzah, who then drops dead (verses 6–7). Eugene Peterson, outlining the slow drips of disobedience and spiritual carelessness over years that led to this point, says of Uzzah: 'this was not sudden death: it was slow suicide.'[4]

The choices we make about God and the things of God have consequences on our spiritual life expectancy, just as the choices we make about diet and exercise have consequences on our physical life expectancy. While Peter was motivated out of natural, understandable cowardice, Ananias and Sapphira were motivated out of greed and a compulsion to deceive. Although Peter's offence seems so much more heinous on the surface, Peter's heart and Ananias' heart were worlds apart. A minor sin out of a cold, scheming, unrepentant heart is so much more serious than a major offence honestly confessed. It is never the size of the sin that matters, but the depth of God's grace.

The saddest thing about the story is that it didn't need to be that way. This couple had plenty of opportunity to live as authentic disciples: they were part of the community, they had a chance. Right up to the end they had the chance to repent and they didn't take it. They followed the example of Judas rather than Peter; the road to destruction rather than that of repentance and restoration.

4 Eugene Peterson, 'Why did Uzzah die? Why did David dance?', Convocation Address, May 1995, *Regent College* (Regent College Audio, Vancouver).

What sort of God?

If this story had been in the Epic of Gilgamesh of the Babylonians, in Greek mythology or even in the Qur'an, we wouldn't be surprised, because the God of the Babylonians, the Greek gods and the Allah of Islam are presented as unpredictable and inscrutable. They can decide on a whim to wipe out whoever they wish. But Christians have a problem because the God of Scripture is different. Immediately after this story we read of healings and miracles, and broken people being restored and given hope (Acts 5:12–16). We see a God who makes people generous and loving, who heals, who releases them from prison, who has a message of new life and forgiveness (Acts 5:17 and the following verses). However, Chapter 5 also serves to fill out the picture; it reminds us that ours is a God to be appropriately feared (verse 11). The aftermath was a very subdued church, but one that was delivered from a poison of greed, deception and hypocrisy that could have proved fatal in its formative years.

PRAY:

Heavenly Father, we praise and thank you for the great depths of your grace. Though we deserve judgment and death, you have offered us forgiveness and life through your Son. We praise you also for being a perfect and righteous judge and for protecting your kingdom and your gospel message. Forgive us, we ask, for the times that we have not responded to your grace and not trusted you and your ways. Protect us from a hard, unrepenting heart and continue to teach us to fear you. We pray along with your servant David that you would search us and know our hearts, and that you would test us and know our thoughts. In your kindness, lead us out of all wickedness and into your everlasting way of life (Psalm 139:23–24). In your Son's name, we pray this in faith. Amen.

CRAIG WEYRENS – IFES EUROPE ASSOCIATE
REGIONAL SECRETARY

THE WIDER STORY

READ: ACTS 5:12 – 6:7

Chapter 5:12–16 summarizes a ministry of remarkable healings and exorcisms which led to the apostles being held in great esteem and treated with awe by the people. This in turn led to jealousy and rage from the High Priest and his allies (verses 17–26), as it had done with Jesus himself. The apostles are imprisoned, but miraculously freed; they are told to cease preaching, but refuse. (Interestingly, verse 29 has provided the classic Christian basis for civil disobedience over the centuries.) In the end, although they are beaten, they are saved from further punishment through the pragmatic intervention of one of the Jewish leaders, Gamaliel, a mentor to Saul of Tarsus (verses 33–40). So the disciples continue to preach fearlessly (verse 42), their courage proving to be the inspiration for thousands of persecuted Christians in history who learn to view their suffering as a badge of honour (verse 41).

Chapter 6 begins with a case study in church governance and wisdom. The apostles choose seven men (deacons) to assist the apostles. But it is no simple division between 'spiritual' and 'practical' ministry. These seven also needed to be of good reputation, full of the Holy Spirit and wisdom. The fact that Stephen was one of these seven demonstrates that this was no second-class ministry, as we will see in the next story.

REFLECT:

- In what areas may you need to 'obey God rather than human beings' (Acts 5:29)?
- What would your response be if you were 'ordered … not to speak in the name of Jesus' (Acts 5:40)?
- The apostles rejoiced that they had been 'counted worthy of suffering disgrace for the Name' of Jesus (Acts 5:41). Reflect on this and pray for courage in any opposition you may be facing because of your Christian faith.

AN EVENING PSALM

READ: PSALM 63

David spent many years in the wilderness. He knew what it was to be thirsty (verse 1) and surrounded by troubles (verses 9–10). But in the centre of the psalm we find the key to his resilience. His past times of worship sustain him; he knows the glory and power of his God (verses 2–5) and even now in this desert place he will cling to him (verses 6–8). The end of the psalm (verses 9–11) reminds us of this morning's readings and how those who are a threat to the integrity of God's people will eventually face his judgment: 'the mouths of liars will be silenced' (verse 11). But God's judgment on all that spoils his world and his church is set in the context of his mercy and grace towards those who love him. The problem with David's enemies – and with Ananias and Sapphira – was that they never earnestly sought God (verses 1–2). If they had, they would have known the truth of verse 3. Reread this psalm slowly and ask yourself how your past experiences of God's goodness will sustain you in the desert times. When we believe that God's love is indeed 'better than life' (verse 3), then we have nothing to fear.

DAY 20

MISSION & MARTYRDOM

READ: ACTS 6:8 – 7:8, 44–60

*Now Stephen, a man full of God's grace and power,
performed great wonders and signs among the
people. Opposition arose, however ...*

ACTS 6:8–9

Mission in the name of Jesus will bring opposition,
ridicule, possibly persecution and sometimes death. The
experience of Stephen, one of 'the seven' who had been
chosen mainly for practical ministry within the church
(6:1–7), illustrates this. He was the first Christian martyr.
But it has always been true since Jesus first predicted it,
saying to his disciples that a time would come when
they would 'be handed over to be persecuted and put to
death' (Matthew 24:9). It has also been the experience
of many students and student ministries over the years.
Charles Simeon ministered in Cambridge, UK in the late
nineteenth century and many university students came
to faith through his preaching. Yet he was barred from
taking services in his own church and students who were
challenged by his preaching and came to Christ were
ostracized, ridiculed and, on at least one occasion, denied
academic prizes because of their beliefs. Vandalism to his
church went unpunished and was even believed to have
been encouraged by others within the church hierarchy.

This was Stephen's experience too, opposed by the
religious authorities of the day. Their accusations were that he
was against the Temple and the Law. Basically, he wasn't 'part
of their group' and he didn't obey their rules (see Acts 6:13).

When Stephen gets the chance to defend himself, he begins a long speech which we may find hard, or even tedious, to read. On the surface it seems to be a long history lesson and if that is not 'your thing', you could easily skip over it. But with only a limited amount of parchment to write his book of Acts, Luke thinks it important enough to give us over fifty verses of his speech. Why? It is because the speech reminds us of several vital things concerning how God works with his people.

We have a God who knows no boundaries

Stephen was accused of being 'against [the Temple]' (6:13). So he shows that God was never limited to a building (7:48). He cites how God spoke to Abraham in pagan Mesopotamia, Isaac and Jacob when they were wandering ancient Judea (7:2–8), Joseph in Egypt and Moses in the desert of Midian (7:9–43). He also states how God spoke through the prophets in a variety of places (7:52).

We have a God who is faithful through history

Stephen also highlights that God kept his promise to Abraham: he kept Joseph and Moses safe in the household of a foreign king, and he kept them going at times of imprisonment and rebellion.

God's faithful people obey where God leads and give what God asks

Faithful followers are prepared to pay the ultimate price and go the ultimate distance. Abraham heard and obeyed; Joseph kept his integrity regardless of the cost; Moses persevered with an ungrateful people; and the prophets spoke although they were rejected and stoned. Now Stephen, with his life in the balance, is still prepared to witness for Christ.

I once heard an African pastor say to a group of Western churches who were constantly being tempted to change their position on the authority of Scripture, the uniqueness of Jesus and the biblical requirements for believers in areas of sexuality and identity: 'Don't start compromising in the West on issues for which we in the developing world are laying down our lives!'

Luke's main concern in this chapter is not so much the martyrdom of Stephen, but the spread of the church. The two were of course related. By his teaching and example of faithfulness to the point of death, Stephen facilitates the worldwide spread of the church. While mission led to martyrdom in the case of Stephen, in terms of God's ultimate purposes, martyrdom also led to mission – as the apostles were scattered and preached wherever they went.

And Stephen was rewarded. What? By being stoned? No, but there was a reward nonetheless. He got a glimpse none of us will probably ever have, because it is only natural and right that God would reserve such things for those at the extremities of their natural ability to persevere. Like a marathon runner is kept going by the thought of his family waiting at the finishing line to celebrate, Stephen is given a glimpse of heaven and of Jesus standing to acknowledge his arrival and welcome him home.

Stephen could have saved his skin, tempered his words diplomatically or kept quiet altogether, but he knew what was at stake: the very integrity of the radical message of Jesus – the gospel itself. If he had compromised on *anything* here, if he had said that some of the Law was still necessary to be right with God, or that some temple-worship in a particular geographical place was necessary to be a true God-fearer, if he had made any such concessions, the Christian faith would have been finished. Because those two things go right to the heart of all that Jesus came to do. He died to set us free from the Law. He died to give us free access to the Father.

The end of this chapter sounds worse than a bad parliamentary debate in most of our countries, with various parties shouting over each other. Out of this chaos, justice was never going to be possible in this life. Yet Stephen's love, even for his murderers, is not in doubt. He dies with words of forgiveness on his lips (verse 60). But he would not compromise on the gospel or on the glory of God!

A student story

In 2015, terrorists from Somalia came south to the Kenyan city of Garissa. Knowing that all the Islamic students would be at prayer and anyone still on campus would be Christian, they killed 148 of the Christian students. Many were at a prayer meeting run by the IFES group on campus. Four years later I had the joy of reading an application for financial help from the Christian Union in that university who wanted help for a program aimed specifically at building bridges and sharing their faith with Muslim students. Last year 5,000 Christian students gathered in Kenya for a mission conference. One student testified that ten of his university friends had come to faith that year. From the embers of a great persecution the renewed fire of revival had started to burn.

PRAY:

Our God and Father, throughout history you have taught us what it means to follow you, what it means to carry our cross – a cross that you yourself carried under the mockery and rejection of your own. Lord, you did not spare yourself from rejection and persecution to the point of death. The way you chose to give us life – life in abundance – challenges us and sometimes disturbs us. Later, other men and women of faith followed you on this path. They did not spare their lives to announce your truth and glorify your name among their people. From the time of Stephen until today, from Jerusalem to the ends of the earth, your children sometimes pay a high price to belong to you and remain faithful to you. As with Stephen, you have given them the faith and strength to remain faithful to you in these times of trial. Today, Lord, teach us to be inspired by their example of perseverance and faithfulness. May we, as a universal church, keep them in our prayers and remain faithful to you. In the name of Jesus, we pray, Amen.

JAMIL – REGIONAL SECRETARY FOR THE MIDDLE EAST AND NORTH AFRICA

THE WIDER STORY

READ: ACTS 7:9–43

Acts 7:9–43 fills out the story of Joseph through to the people of Israel's rebellion in the wilderness and the prophecy of their exile. Read it with an eye on the points mentioned above: God's patience with his people and how he spoke to them in many different places.

REFLECT:

- What does Stephen's recap of Israel's history tell us about God's character?
- How does it broaden your perspective on God's purposes?
- What encouragement can you take from Stephen's speech?

AN EVENING PSALM

READ: PSALM 116

Verse 15 of this psalm reminds us how precious to the Lord is the death of any of his people. It is not the end; it is a homecoming like that experienced by Stephen in his vision that we read about this morning. It is the moment when, having watched over them for a short time on this earth, the Lord brings his precious child home to share eternity with him. The psalm is mainly a song of thanks to God for his protection while the psalmist is 'in the land of the living' (verse 9). He recounts the many incidents when his prayers for protection were answered (verses 1–2, 4, 6, 8) and how he vowed to live a life of obedience in response to God's mercy (verses 9, 12–14), particularly in his commitment to worship God faithfully.

But these thanksgivings have limitations; they are temporal. He knows he is not going to live forever, regardless of how many times God rescues him in this life. There is a reference to 'as long as …' in verse 2, but that time will pass. So the psalm acknowledges the reality of death (verses 15, and possibly 7). Stephen understood this well enough to know that even when his time came, the Lord would be there to welcome his servant home. Whether you have suffered the bereavement of a close Christian relative or friend, or whether you still harbour some fears of death, be assured tonight that the Lord regards his 'saints' as children of immense value who are dear to him, and that he will protect you until the day when he receives you to himself.

IN THE REVIVAL AND IN THE DESERT

READ: ACTS 8:1–8, 26–40

Now an angel of the Lord said to Philip, 'Go south to the road – the desert road.'

ACTS 8:26

It was a dangerous time to be a Christian. One of their respected leaders had just been stoned to death, and now we read that a great persecution has broken out and the church is scattered (verses 1–2). At the head of the terror gang was Saul who was dragging off and destroying Christians like a wild animal with its prey (verses 2–3). Young or old, woman or man, no one was safe.

If the church was merely a human institution, this alone would have been enough to end it before it had barely begun. In a tactic used by tyrannical governments all over the world, the Christians were divided and dispersed throughout the known world. Surely there was no way these communities could survive, or their message be believed? They would be dispirited and scared to open their mouths! But no! As they were scattered, they 'preached the word wherever they went' (verse 4). This could have been a death sentence for them, but as we saw three days ago, they couldn't help it; they couldn't keep this amazing life-giving, life-changing message to themselves.

In February 2022, many were shocked to see Russia invading its neighbour Ukraine and beginning a series of deadly attacks in the east of the country and on the capital Kyiv. While many stayed to defend their country, others fled for safety, among them many Christians and staff and students of 'CCX', the strong and vibrant IFES movement in Ukraine. Within a matter of weeks we were hearing reports of people turning to Christ as a result of the witness of these courageous Christians. Fleeing Ukrainians and people in the neighbouring countries of Poland, Romania and Belarus, were responding in greater numbers to the message of hope the gospel offered. Dispersion had brought with it new opportunities for witness and proclamation.

Things may not turn out as we wish, but God still goes before us

Like those Ukrainians 2,000 years later, Philip learned that even out of the darkness of death and persecution God had significant plans for him. He ended up in Samaria, the territory of the traditional enemy of Israel, and not somewhere that would have been top of a Jew's list of travel destinations. But Philip (possibly because he was of Greek background), found that he had a ready audience prepared to hear the message. If we look back at Acts 6:1–6 we see that the recently martyred Stephen and Philip were two of 'the seven' who were chosen for ministries of practical service so that the apostles could devote themselves to prayer and preaching (6:4). Yet it is these humble men (today, we would call them 'deacons') who were not primarily evangelists, apologists or healers, but are called to be the great evangelists, apologists and healers in these early chapters of Acts.

No matter what our main area of ministry may be, no matter what our individual gifts or strengths may be in any test, tool or metric we may take, every one of us is called to be an evangelist; to be ready to obey the call of Christ, to bring healing to disturbed hearts and minds and to 'always be prepared … to give the reason for the hope that [we] have' within us (1 Peter 3:15). The rest of this chapter shows how God continues to lead his people not just in times of difficulty, but also when things are going well.

We may not end up where we want to be, but God will still use us

Philip didn't choose Samaria. Like the exiled refugee Ukrainians he was a 'victim of circumstance'. But look how God used him in this new place of exile. The people paid close attention, saw the miracles and there was 'great joy' in the city (verses 6–8). We may have our preferred places of ministry or contexts where we think we will be more at home: our 'comfort zone'. But we make a massive mistake if we think that our comfort zones and our 'used by God zones' are the same thing. One of the most spectacular revivals in the early church took place as a result of persecution, by the preaching of someone who wasn't a preacher, and at a place where none of the apostles would have been particularly comfortable. But it happened because one man was open to God's leading and was so gripped by the gospel that he shared it wherever he went.

We must be ready to serve 'the one' as well as 'the many'

After the trauma of persecution and God's wonderful providence in establishing a new arena for ministry, we might think Philip should expect God to give him some time to 'catch his breath'; a period of stability, perhaps to do some Samaritan follow-up and discipleship. However,

God calls him away from the scene of his most fruitful work to go to a desert road and to speak to one person. Someone who, as a eunuch and a Gentile, would have been doubly excluded from the Old Testament people. But now a different kingdom was emerging – a fulfilment of the vision of Isaiah 56:3–5 (from the same scroll that this eunuch was reading) where eunuchs could find healing and hope. God had been at work in this influential government official. Soon he was going to read of that hope in Chapter 56, but first he needed to be introduced to the one whose sacrificial death opened the way for him to be included. So he was reading Isaiah Chapter 53. All he needed was someone to explain it to him.

The student population is one of the most globally mobile. Every year thousands of internationals come to our universities all over the world and hundreds of 'Philips' sit and explain the Good News of Jesus to them. All boundaries of nationality, race and sexuality are broken in Christ, as women and men find their primary identity in him.

Acts 8 shows us that God can achieve his purposes out of the darkness of persecution as much as in the heat of a revival. Similarly, while God can work among the crowds, he is equally interested in the one person in the desert. Philip was prepared to be used in both contexts. Even though it wasn't his 'sweet spot', he was prepared to stand in front of a crowd and face the powers of evil when he needed to. He also didn't let a successful public ministry go to his head. He didn't think it was 'beneath him' to leave the limelight to minister to one seeking soul. There can be no egos in Christian ministry. If we truly want to be used by God we need to praise him in the desert as well as in the revival; we need to bring him to the 'one' as well as to 'the many'.

PRAY:

Dear Lord, we acknowledge that you are a God of revival and also a God of desert places. There is nothing beyond your knowledge and power. Today we pray that you will be with all of us as we pass through desert and persecution at the hands of so many that would destroy the truth of your Word. Help us to find your purposes in the midst of our desert. God, I also pray for the families whose lives are fractured by war and whose hearts ache for their loved ones. Please give them strength and let them know that you are there for them in such a difficult time. Help us to humble ourselves to follow your call and guidance, even if it takes us out of our comfort zone. Grant us your grace to be flexible and obey your lead. In Jesus' name, Amen!

ZELALEM ABEBE – REGIONAL SECRETARY, ENGLISH-& PORTUGUESE-SPEAKING AFRICA

THE WIDER STORY

READ: ACTS 8:9–25

Verses 9–25 tell us of the visit of Peter and John to Samaria to witness first-hand the coming of the Holy Spirit on the Samaritans. For John, particularly, this was a transformative experience. In Luke 9:54 he wanted to see a very different sort of fire fall on the Samaritans (see Day 7). A well-known magician sees events and, for a while, seems to have joined the fellowship. However, his subsequent request to 'buy the Holy Spirit' puts him closer to the confidence tricksters of modern religious TV channels than to genuine disciples. He is an example that neither words of vague testimony nor even baptism (however it is administered) guarantees regeneration.

REFLECT:

- John's view of Samaritans has radically changed since Luke Chapter 9. When have you had to repent of your attitude towards people whom God has accepted?
- Simon stands as a warning to all who have unworthy ambitions or try to buy influence within the church. Are there ambitions or wrong motivations that you need to repent of? Have there ever been times where, like Simon, you have wanted to use spiritual things to your own advantage?

AN EVENING PSALM

READ: PSALM 43

This psalm was probably originally part of Psalm 42, which you might like to read (see how verse 5 repeats the chorus of 42:11). Both are psalms of someone in despair and even in depression. In these situations it is common to talk to ourselves; we listen to voices from within and the messages are rarely helpful. Here, at a time when he is truly disturbed, the psalmist uses his inner conversation to reorientate himself: 'put your hope in God' (42:11; 43:5). He looks to the future, to a time when he will once again be able to worship him: 'I will yet praise him' (42:11; 43:5). That time may not be now, but he aims for it.

Why can he be so confident? Because he has taken refuge in the right place: not in artificial and temporary cures or false 'saviours' but in God (verse 2). In the middle of his oppression, he has asked God to send his 'light and [his] truth' (verse 3, ESV). That light for guidance and truth for assurance will lead him back to God's presence in a deeper way. The Ethiopian we read about this morning would have experienced the fulfilment of verses 3–4. Having come to worship God with only partial knowledge, his encounter with Philip brought him greater light and truth in answer to his simple prayer. I have met many students who struggle in the darkness and who are listening to the wrong inner voices. Meditate on this psalm and pray that God's light and truth would bring you from pain to praise.

PEOPLE *CAN* CHANGE!

READ: ACTS 9:1–19

He fell to the ground and heard a voice say to him, 'Saul, Saul, why do you persecute me?'

ACTS 9:4

The history of Christianity would have been very different without this episode. One of the greatest enemies of Christians, full of religious zeal and self-righteous fervour, is brought to his knees, literally, and becomes the most influential figure in the early church. Saul was a relentless terrorist (see Acts 8:3) and, not content with Jerusalem, he now wanted to expand his empire of executions to Damascus. There was only one thing on his mind that day: killing. If you were a young Christian, Damascus wasn't safe. Places of worship weren't safe; women weren't safe; there was no refuge if you were a follower of Jesus.

So what happened? The phrase 'Damascus road experience' is used in many cultures to denote a complete change of worldview. But, powerful though it is, we need to beware of making this story a template of all conversions. I have heard seeking students and others casually say that they are waiting for their 'Damascus road experience'. I feel like replying: 'Well, if you want the genuine experience you probably first need to breathe out murderous threats, raid a few synagogues, kick a few doors down, beat up a few women and drag a bunch of Christians off to prison – because that's what the original "Damascus road experience" was reserved for!'

For most of us, our experience is much more Peter than Saul. Peter had multiple enlightenments in his years as a young disciple (Matthew 16:16; John 21:15; even Acts 10 – see Day 23). Yet both Peter and Saul's experiences were supernatural. In both cases, God, by his Holy Spirit, is changing them from who they were into who they were made to be. Nevertheless, when you take away the spectacular blinding light and the voice, Saul's conversion contains at least three things that are essential for anyone who wants to become a follower of Christ.

From arrogance to humility

Saul was in no doubt that he was right in what he was doing. He was zealous, and religious zealotry can be the worst kind. You can read about his religious CV in Philippians Chapter 3. But that day he was brought to his knees. In Acts 26, Saul (now Paul), is telling his testimony to King Agrippa and he adds a phrase that Luke leaves out from the narrative in this chapter. Paul says that the voice from heaven said, 'Saul, why do you persecute me? It is hard for you to kick against the goads' (Acts 26:14). The image is of an ox resisting the instructions of its owner and kicking against the sharp stick (goad) that was encouraging it in a certain direction. Jesus was saying to Saul: 'You are resisting what you know to be right and it's only going to get more painful if you keep going. Stop kicking!'

From that moment there was no more kicking and screaming or resistance. All of that was over. The Saul that enters Damascus is a broken and changed man from the one that left Jerusalem. Transformed. In any conversion, whether quiet or spectacular, there needs to be a journey from arrogance to humility. You may not be a murderous zealot; but any feeling that you can live without God, that Jesus' crucifixion was necessary for really bad people like Saul but not for you, is the same arrogance that needs to be dealt with by God's grace.

From power to weakness

Saul was powerful enough to have the ear of the High Priest and demand letters to enable him to continue his persecution; powerful enough, essentially, to be a glorified gang leader and have an entourage of men with him and to arrive like some intimidating militia come to terrorize the neighbourhood; powerful enough to drag people away like wild animals. But what is he at the end? Broken, blind, unable to walk by himself, not eating or drinking. Weak.

Conversion only happens when we let go of whatever power we have, even if – especially if – it is just the most modern of idols: the power over our own lives and our own choices; the power of self-autonomy, self-expression or self-government. Christian conversion only happens when we become weak.

From religion to grace

Saul would have been confident that his theology was right. He believed that God was for Israel and it was the role of all other nations to obey Israel's God and follow Israel's rules and he was there to preserve and protect the purity and power of Israel. Tragically, there are too many places in the world today where Christians believe this is their primary calling – they just replace the word 'Israel' with the name of their country.

It was on the Damascus road that Saul realized his religious CV counted for nothing (Philippians 3:7).

Conversion is by grace alone. God could only use a broken and humbled Saul; and he can only use us when we are empty of all self-importance, self-identity and self-righteousness and replace them with God-importance, God-identity and God-righteousness.

A reluctant hero

But Saul is not the only person who is changed in this chapter. This Ananias (not the Ananias we encountered in Day 19, a different person entirely) was willing to believe that the Gospel *can* change people. He obeys the vision he has received and he goes to find and seek out this man who had come to Damascus to find and seek him out!

This Ananias is chosen by God for one of the most important ministries we see in the New Testament. It was no Day of Pentecost sermon, but he speaks two words that were probably as powerful in their effect as any sermon preached by any apostle: 'Brother Saul' (Acts 9:17)! Can you imagine the effect those two words would have had on the man who would only have expected rejection and even revenge from the people he had persecuted? He experienced this same grace from Barnabas later (see Acts 11:19–26).

A student story

Gabriel, a graduate in DRC, was a nurse who decided to mobilize for mission the churches in his war zone. As he was standing at the pulpit, he was kidnapped by insurgents and taken to the jungles of Congo. For a week he witnessed how innocent civilians were slaughtered and others suffered sexual violence and slavery. As he knew he was a candidate for murder, he decided to share the love of God with the rebels' commander. This miraculously gave him a breakthrough to share that love of God further, in three rebel camps, and the commander and sixty-three rebels committed themselves to Christ. The commander, with tears, would introduce Gabriel's sermons saying, 'Come and listen to what no man who came here ever told me'. When Gabriel was released, the commander, together with ten other rebels, decided to surrender their guns and the UN led them back to their country. Let us never limit God!

PRAY:

Dear Father, thank you that you are my Father and I am your child. With your Holy Spirit, you are changing me from who I was into who I was made to be. You know everything about me, you see my heart and thoughts. Thank you for all the transformations that are already happening in my life because of the work of your Spirit. I want to be the vessel through which you will show your love. Please cleanse me. Where I am arrogant, where I think of myself higher than others, make me humble. Where I rely on my power and my knowledge, make me one who trusts in your strength. Where I am full of self-conceit and self-satisfaction, make me one who sees through your eyes. Lord, help me hear to whom you are sending me today. Who is the person who needs to be inspired, supported, hugged and called a brother or sister today? Use me as your vessel. Amen.

LARISA GORELOVA-LOBOVA – STAFF, GEORGIA, EURASIA REGION

THE WIDER STORY

READ: ACTS 9:20–43

The rest of Chapter 9 charts Paul's acceptance by the early church in Damascus and Jerusalem after their initial scepticism (see verses 21, 26). Paul's clear conversion and powerful testimony and teaching leaves the church astounded and they are instrumental in saving his life as his previous allies threaten to kill him (verses 25, 30). Barnabas ('son of encouragement' – Acts 4:36) is reintroduced in verse 27 as a major factor in Paul's integration into the Christian community. Verse 31 is another of those memorable summary verses of how the early church was strengthened and grew. Verses 32–43 switch the spotlight to Peter and two of his major miracles: the healing of Aeneas and resurrection of Dorcas.

REFLECT:

- To whom could you be an encouraging 'Barnabas'?
- What characterized the church in verse 31? Which of those qualities do you and your church need today?

AN EVENING PSALM

READ: PSALM 30

As a student of the Scriptures, Saul would have known this psalm well. But after his experience on the road to Damascus it would have assumed a whole new depth of meaning for him. That day he would know what it was to be 'lifted out of the depths' (verse 3) and brought out of spiritual death and darkness. He would particularly have understood the truth of verse 5. God's response to Saul's persecution was to confront him in power at that 'moment' on the Damascus road and change him for a lifetime. This is a psalm of transformation: from experiencing God's righteous anger to benefitting from his grace and mercy; from weeping to rejoicing (verse 5); from wailing to dancing; from sackcloth to joy (verse 11). We may not have experienced a dramatic conversion like Saul did, but all of us have been brought from the depths of our own sin and rebellion to a lifetime of God's favour. *The Message* finishes this Psalm by saying 'I can't thank you enough!' (verse 12). Spend the last few moments of this day in thanksgiving for your new life in Christ and all that he has done for you.

NO ONE IS UNCLEAN

READ: ACTS 10:1 – 11:4

> *I now realize how true it is that God does not show favouritism but accepts from every nation the one who fears him and does what is right.*

ACTS 10:34–35

As we saw yesterday, Paul had a dramatic conversion. For Peter it was more gradual. We need to be careful about making our conversion experience the norm for everyone. Peter had many times of enlightenment in the Scriptures (see Matthew 16; John 21). This is his latest 'conversion'. The story is not just about what God did in Cornelius's life, it is also about Peter's conversion to a fuller understanding of the gospel.

God and Cornelius – 'God does not show favouritism' (Acts 10:34)

This God-fearing Gentile is visited supernaturally and eventually led to Peter and to the truth. God was at work in Cornelius's life long before he met Peter and before he actually heard the gospel message. At this stage no Christian would consider sharing this news with him because the Christians were all Jews and the Jews didn't associate with Gentiles. So God intervenes supernaturally. When Christians are not obedient, God's ways will not be thwarted and he will still find ways of extending his kingdom among those we ignore or even despise. Just as God was working in Cornelius's life before he met Peter or heard the gospel, God is at work in all sorts of places on our campuses, preparing the ground for all of us to go and 'do a Peter' and preach the message into that fertile spiritual soil. *When the Holy Spirit is at work, 'outsiders' are brought in regardless of the obedience or receptiveness of Christians.*

God and Peter – 'Do not call anything impure' (Acts 10:15)

Often in our Christian lives, in our ministry, and even in our mission, we need to re-evaluate. Peter had to learn that some of his traditions about not associating with Gentiles were not biblical but cultural – and actually wrong! They needed to be ditched! The gospel was more important and living out gospel principles became the priority. *When the Holy Spirit is at work, 'insiders' are forced to question and re-evaluate what is really important.*

Peter and Cornelius – 'It is against our law … to associate' (Acts 10:28)

Peter doesn't just get up and preach. He starts by sharing what God has been doing in *his* life. He is personal, humble and vulnerable. 'It is against our law for a Jew to associate with [you]' (verse 28). But it wasn't! The 'law' here, is not the biblical Old Testament Law, but a cultural taboo. In another version, Peter says, 'You know, I'm sure that this is highly irregular. Jews just don't do this – visit and relax with people of another race' (verses 27–29, MSG). Whatever cultural baggage or prejudices we may have that could prevent us from going to certain areas or talking to certain people must be laid aside. We must get rid of whatever unwritten or unspoken rules exist within our community – those that keep us from other people

– if we are to be beacons of light in the darkness of our culture. The bringing in of God's kingdom of justice and peace is too important for us to be distracted by social expectations, cultural taboos, or what other people might think. *When the Holy Spirit is at work, we must not allow our cultural baggage to hinder the spread of the Good News.*

The Holy Spirit at work – 'They have received ... just as we have' (Acts 10:47)

The Holy Spirit is not dependent on us. The Spirit fell on the believers before Peter finished his evangelistic talk; he continued his work independently of Peter. Peter played his part, but he needed to see that this was not about him. This was not Peter converting Cornelius to his way of thinking, this was Peter and Cornelius both being obedient to God and both finding God in new and unexpected ways.

Notice how the Holy Spirit is a God of *surprises* (verse 45). Notice too how he *breaks down barriers* (verses 45–46). Sometimes secondary things such as culture or religious practice or politics get out of proportion and become things which divide, hurt and exclude. These Jews, it says, were amazed that the Spirit had fallen 'even on the Gentiles' (ESV). For them, this was a bitter pill to swallow. That little word 'even' betrays the fact that they had thought some people to be totally beyond the grace of God.

However, above all, the Holy Spirit *unites*! There is no difference between Jew and Gentile: the same Spirit, the same baptism, the same message, the same cross, the same Christ, the same hope of heaven – for Jews *and* Gentiles. In Christ there is neither one race nor the other, there is a new family. In this family we have more in common with fellow believers who may be different from us in politics, religious background, culture, colour, socio-economic status and education, than we do with unbelievers within our own community or even our own biological family. Jesus has radically redefined family, society and community. *That* was why he died!

Peter and his peers – '[They] criticised him' (Acts 11:2)

Not everyone will appreciate what you try to do in breaking down barriers for the gospel. At times, you will be misunderstood and perhaps all sorts of rumours or conspiracy theories will emerge against you, with some people thinking you have an agenda other than the desire to share the gospel. After the spiritual 'high' of Chapter 10, Peter has to deal with critics within his own community in Chapter 11. Gospel faithfulness will involve opposition, misunderstanding and explanation.

Often student movements have been beacons of hope and light in countries or regions where communities are torn apart and even the churches are divided along cultural or political lines. In Ireland, for example, the IFES movement comprises both North and South; in the Balkans, the leaders of the Serbian and Albanian movements are close friends, and have worked tirelessly to demonstrate the reconciling power of the gospel even though they have lost friends from their own community by doing so. In Israel, the movement consists of students from Arab and Hebrew backgrounds and the General Secretary of the movement and the Chair of the Board are always from different communities. Similar stories of reconciliation could be told from Sri Lanka and the United States. Often there is a cost, as with Peter, because many in the churches will disagree or even oppose such work. Might God be challenging *you* to confess prejudice or lead others in reaching out across barriers our cultures have erected?

PRAY:

> *Holy Spirit, my heart's cry is that, like Cornelius, like Peter, I will set apart time to dwell in your presence and to pray. Grow within me my heart's desire to be shaped into the likeness of Jesus, and as I kneel before you, I bring to you who I have become: through the influences of the years gone by; through the dominant conversations and practices; in the homes of my family and friends; in my formative years at school and now in my university; in our communities, the media and the arts.*
>
> *Speak your kingdom truths into who I have become.*
>
> *Thank you for all that is of you.*
>
> *Bring to the surface, Lord, anything that I have believed to be true but is not, and give me the courage to change course in keeping with your kingdom truths. Let me be your eyes, your ears, your voice, your hands and your feet, bringing reconciliation and justice.*
>
> *May the meditation of my heart be acceptable and pleasing in your sight.*
>
> *May your glory endure forever, Amen.*

SAVITHRI SUMANTHIRA – REGIONAL SECRETARY, SOUTH ASIA

THE WIDER STORY

READ: ACTS 11:1 – 14:28

A lot happens between Chapters 11 and 15. Acts 11:19–30 tells of missionary activity, prophecy and famine relief by the disciples (many of them nameless) and how the church grew in Antioch (modern-day Syria) under the teaching of Barnabas and Paul. It was there the word 'Christian' was first used. There are two notable speeches: Peter explaining the work among the Gentiles (11:4–18) and Paul's sermon in Antioch (in Pisidia, 13:13–43) which has a lot of echoes of Stephen's speech in Chapter 7. Luke is determined that his readers understand that Christianity was no new sect but the fulfilment of all foretold in the Scriptures. But these chapters also develop the twin themes of the growth of the church and its persecution by both Jewish and Gentile leaders. King Herod kills the apostle James (12:1–3) and imprisons Peter who is then miraculously delivered (12:4–19) before Herod himself suffers God's judgment (12:20–23).

Chapters 13–14 recount what is known as 'Paul's first missionary journey'. After Paul and Barnabas are commissioned, they set out for Cyprus and we read of initial success (13:5–12, 42–44, 48–49) but plenty of opposition (13:45–47, 50). This pattern is repeated in Iconium (14:1–7). Similarly, in Lystra (14:8–18) there is a miraculous healing and a speech by Paul as he stops the crowd from worshipping them. This is followed by a serious attempt on Paul's life as he is stoned and left for dead (14:19). However, there appears to have been a miraculous recovery as the disciples gather round him (presumably praying) and the rest of the chapter consists of Paul and Barnabas strengthening the new believers in the region: warning them of persecution, encouraging them to remain steadfast, and planting churches, before returning home and reporting on how God was at work among the Gentiles (14:20–28).

REFLECT:

- What can we learn about mission from this cycle of conversions and opposition?
- What can we learn from the apostles' response to opposition?
- How can Acts 14:22 help you persevere in your own discipleship and mission?

AN EVENING PSALM

READ: PSALM 104

This is a psalm that celebrates God's creative genius. The first part praises him for the pleasure his creation gives to all who share it. Whether you are a zoologist, an ornithologist, a vintner or a sailor – there is something here for you. God has made an amazing world for us to enjoy, which is why we are to hate anything that robs us of that joy or spoils that creation. The second part of the psalm concentrates on God's sovereignty over all the thousands of creatures and species that surround us; God owns it all. This was the lesson Peter learned in this morning's reading and he had to apply it to how he regarded and treated other people. God is creator and sustainer (verses 24–26, 27–30). Even though we have exploited the things he has given us and our ecology is broken, still God in his grace 'renew[s] the face of the ground' (verse 30). The psalm finishes by marvelling at the power of God. This amazing creative and sustaining

God deserves lifelong praise. The final verse seems harsh. In the immediate context it is a prayer that those who rebel against this sovereign God and spoil his creation would be judged. But it is also a reminder for us today that all of us 'sinners' would face that judgment ourselves if it were not for the provision made by God himself through Christ. Tonight, thank God for this amazing provision and also for the beauty of the world he has created for us to enjoy.

NO BARRIERS

READ: ACTS 15:1-29

God, who knows the heart, showed that he accepted them by giving the Holy Spirit to them just as he did to us. He did not discriminate between us and them, for he purified their hearts by faith.

ACTS 15:8-9

Few people get excited about organizational politics, church governance, constitutions and legal processes. Sometimes those who do enjoy it are the last people you want involved! The problem is that when disputes arise it is necessary to have good procedures in place to deal with them in a godly manner. Similarly, not everyone enjoys theological debate or discussion, or regards it as important. They feel it would be much easier if we just 'got along together' and accepted our differences. The problem is that some issues *are* important; in fact, some are essential to keeping the church alive.

If two doctors disagree on a diagnosis and treatment, and following one doctor's advice will cure the patient while the other will kill her, then forgetting the differences and respecting both opinions is not good enough! It is why the early church formulated creeds and confessions; it is why organizations such as IFES have a Doctrinal Basis as a statement of unity around essentials whilst maintaining diversity on secondary matters. In Acts Chapter 15 we are faced with the first really serious theological debate in the early church and we get a glimpse into how the apostles settled such matters.

The issue

Some were teaching that circumcision was essential to being saved (verse 1). It was clear that Paul and Barnabas disagreed with them because the dispute was sharp and intense and resulted in them travelling to Jerusalem to get consensus from the other apostles (verse 2). But notice that, before this took place, Paul and Barnabas were spreading the word of what God had been doing among the Gentiles (verses 3–4). It is likely that our New Testament book of Galatians, which deals with this very issue, was written at this time (between the events recounted in verses 1 and 3).

The process

The apostles heard both sides (verses 5–7). They listened to personal testimony as Peter reported what had happened to him in yesterday's reading (verses 7–11), and as Paul and Barnabas reported back from their missionary journey (verse 12). They then considered how this tallied with Scripture, as James pointed to the prophecies concerning the salvation of the Gentiles (verses 13–18).

The conclusion

The issue was not resolved by Peter or James giving an authoritative verdict but by consensus, having listened for the Holy Spirit's leading (verse 8). They dealt with the primary issue while agreeing to compromise on secondary issues for the sake of unity in the church. So they decreed that the Gentiles should not be required to be circumcised. This was theological – because God had already accepted them on equal terms (verses 9, 11). It was also practical – because strict adherence to the Law of Moses had been far too heavy a burden for even the Jews to bear (verse 10).

This was a decision which would be difficult for many Jewish Christians to accept, but it was essential if Gentile converts were ever to be regarded as equals, and, for Paul and the others, this was right at the heart of the gospel (see Galatians 3:28). If the apostles had not had the courage to make this decision, then the church would have been divided and its mission would have been stifled right at its birth. The very nature of the church was under attack.

The compromise

Why then did they ask the Gentiles to obey some laws (verses 20, 29)? This is an example of how churches and organizations sometimes have to make pragmatic temporary decisions as well as giving clarification on important matters of doctrine. In this case, these directions were concessions to the Jews so that Jew-Gentile fellowship meals could continue. Most of the requests had to do with dietary laws. If the Jews had to learn to embrace their uncircumcised Gentile brothers, then the Gentiles needed to forgo some of their freedoms to keep the fellowship with Jews and not offend their consciences. This is a good example of gracious compromise on 'secondary' matters once the 'primary matter' had been clarified. In addition, as a reminder, the Gentiles were told to be particularly vigilant in avoiding sexual sin, which would have been a constant danger in many of the over-sexualized pagan cultures in which the Gentile converts were living.

So what can we learn?

Doctrine matters

This was not a matter of personal preference. If circumcision had been demanded, then, as the book of Galatians makes clear, the gospel would have been changed and robbed of its power. False teaching has to be opposed or it will be spiritually fatal to impressionable new believers.

Look at issues from the perspective of the outsider

It would have been tempting for the apostles to give in to pressure from their own constituency. The community leaders were powerful, influential and had tradition on their side. Why risk centuries of tradition and offend your own community for the sake of a few outsiders? But the life and ministry of Jesus prove that his heart is for the outsider; he died to bring all nations home. That is what Peter learned and it is what Paul witnessed. Today every Christian community, be it a church or a student group, should always be oriented towards the outsider. Are we placing heavy burdens on seekers or new members: unnecessary behavioural expectations, legalistic regulations, a yoke which we ourselves can't even carry consistently (see verse 10)?

In essentials, unity; in non-essentials, liberty; in all things, charity

History shows that when these three principles are forgotten, problems have arisen in Christian fellowships and between groups. In broad terms there is the tendency both of 'liberal progressives' granting too much liberty in matters of essential doctrine, and 'fundamentalists' not granting enough liberty on secondary matters. In both cases the gospel is diluted and our witness suffers.

This was another landmark moment for the church. It was not as spectacular as a Pentecost sermon, a Damascus road experience or even a Samaritan revival. However, it was crucial to the development of the church along gospel lines. If the apostles had not got their governance processes correct; if they had not studied Scripture or listened to the Holy Spirit; if they had given in to pressure from one lobby group or another – then the Church could have suffered great damage for generations. God can work just as much in committee meetings as in worship gatherings. Pray for those in leadership in your church or fellowship that, like the apostles, they would have wisdom and grace in their decision-making.

PRAY:

Lord, who has gifted us with the costly, gracious gospel! In an uncomfortable world of 'liberal progressives' and hardcore 'fundamentalists', give us servant hearts, that we might be loaded with humility yet unafraid to contend for the gospel. We want to see your gospel undiluted and our witness undeterred. We pray for courage and grace to discern and stand in the midst of a battlefield that would divide us. Grant us openness and critical discernment to weigh what is essential and to advocate liberty in those non-essentials. Lord, in all things, cloak us with your tenacious love and grace. In Jesus' name, we pray, Amen.

ANNETTE ARULRAJAH – REGIONAL SECRETARY, EAST ASIA

THE WIDER STORY

READ: ACTS 15:30 – 16:10

The letter sent from Jerusalem was well received (15:30–35). However, Paul and Barnabas disagree over strategy and team members (15:36–41). This sad division did actually lead to two missionary teams going out: Paul and Silas going one way; Barnabas and John Mark another. In Chapter 16 Paul bravely returns to the Lystra area adding Timothy to the team and, having travelled through and preached in many cities, a vision of a man from Macedonia prompts them to sail there. At this point it seems that Luke himself also joins the team (notice that the 'they' becomes 'we' – Acts 16:10).

REFLECT:

- What can we learn from the disagreement between Paul and Barnabas regarding missionary team work?
- How can Acts 16:6–10 help us deal with situations where our plans have to change or doors seem to be closed to mission?

AN EVENING PSALM

READ: PSALM 98

Acts 15 was all about God's embracing of the nations, treating them equally. The gospel, by the power of the Holy Spirit, was now being preached to the ends of the earth. Psalm 98 celebrates God's rule over all nations (verses 1–2), which he rules with utter justice and equity (verse 9). While Israel knew more of his faithfulness and love, now all the nations would see and experience his salvation (verse 3). The book of Acts is a fulfilment of this psalm – and many others! In the middle, the psalmist simply utters a call to worship. Poetically, he calls all of creation to join in: firstly, humanity created in God's image (verse 4), then musical instruments (verses 5–6) and finally nature itself (verses 7–8), all praising the wonders of this creating, saving God. It is a psalm which should be loved by songwriters, by those working in music and the arts, and those concerned for ecology and conservation. The 'new song' of verse 1 could be a newly written song (as this psalm once was), or it could be one that is new to the singer, or has a new meaning or renewed relevance to the worshipper. What 'new song' has God put on your heart this week? Spend some time thanking him and praising him for his goodness to you.

DAY 25

EXTREME WORSHIP

READ: ACTS 16:11–40

> *About midnight Paul and Silas were praying and singing hymns to God … Suddenly there was such a violent earthquake that the foundations of the prison were shaken … and everyone's chains came loose.*
>
> ACTS 16:25–26

Spam emails are infuriating. Being a Christian leader or pastor may actually mean that you get more than most. A while ago I was encouraged to sign up for a newsletter entitled 'Extreme Worship'. It promised me reviews of all the cutting-edge musical, technological, and audio-visual resources I would need so that my church could enjoy the most 'extreme worship experience'. I wonder what the organization that sent that email would make of the situation in which Paul and Silas found themselves?

The chapter has begun after a disagreement (15:36–41) and continues with disappointments (16:6–7). But God had plans. The apostles receive a special revelation to go to Macedonia, and what happens initially seems very ordinary and unexciting: just a conversation with some women gathered for prayer. But these encounters in Acts 16 can give us an insight into some of the dynamics of mission.

Finding those who are open

Paul and Silas sought out what we might call the 'low-hanging fruit': people who were God-fearing and probably naturally open to listening. We know from other chapters

(13:5, 14; 14:1; 17:1–2) that Paul would normally begin in the synagogue, but, since a synagogue could not be formed without a quota of men, and since those gathered for prayer were all women, it is safe to assume no synagogue existed in Philippi at this time, so he went to the outdoor prayer meeting. This was definitely 'virgin territory' for the gospel.

Patient in the ordinary; ready for the unexpected

They were in Philippi several days before meeting Lydia, and remained there for many days (verses 15, 18). In Athens, Paul's preparatory work took weeks (17:2); in Greece he stayed three months (20:3); and in Corinth his initial ministry took a year and a half (18:11). Acts only gives us the highlights, and naturally it focuses on the spectacular: visions, exorcisms, imprisonments and shipwrecks. But most of the work was done in the small things: the riverside conversations (16:13), midnight evangelistic chats (16:32), the lecture-hall daily discussions (19:9) and the eighteen-month Bible school (18:11). Even after the excitement of the unexpected earthquake, it was the patient teaching of the Word of God that brought the jailer and his family to faith (16:32).

While most of the work is done through these unspectacular ordinary means, Luke shows that, whether it is something routine or unexpected, the Lord is the active agent throughout. He closes doors (verses 6–7); gives visions (verse 9); opens hearts (verse 14); confronts the Enemy and releases the possessed (verse 18); opens mouths in praise (verse 25); and sends earthquakes (verse 26).

A student story

Joshua was a young volunteer working cross-culturally with students in the Middle East. He patiently walked alongside a new friend and shared his life and his faith with him. For months there was no visible sign that the friend was any closer to committing his life to Christ. Then out of the blue, one day, he told Joshua that God had confronted him in a dream and that now this young man realized that all he had seen in Joshua and heard from him was true, and that he was now a believer. Both the patient, ordinary, daily witness of Joshua and the dramatic intervention by God were used in this instance to bring this young student to Christ.

Praising in the pit

What happens when things don't work out? The successes of this story seem overshadowed by the fact that the apostles end up in jail. Circumstances couldn't have been more unfavourable for them: they were called to communicate, yet their message had been misunderstood, deliberately twisted and rejected (verses 19–21); they were called to be itinerant evangelists, yet they were imprisoned and rendered immobile (verses 22–24); they were called to serve the living God, yet it seemed that God had abandoned them.

However, out of this unlikely series of events, and through the apostles' evangelistic worship, a wonderful grace emerges. In spite of the injustice, they *pray*; in spite of the potential mockery of other angry prisoners, they *praise*; in spite of many unanswered questions about God's purposes, they *worship*. And then, in the aftermath of utter chaos, when they could have served their own interests by escaping the situation, they *witness*.

Out of persecution came praise. They sang their way through the chaos and crisis. This was worship that had nothing to do with style, instruments, the intensity of the leader, the beat and rhythm, the length of time songs are sung or how they make you feel. This was *extreme worship*.

They had been misrepresented, lied about, beaten and put into painful stocks in a dark, urine-infested cell, and the first words on their lips were a psalm or a scripture sung in genuine, heartfelt praise to the God who had placed them there for his glory and to achieve his purposes!

The jailer's job was on the line; his reputation was on the line; his life was on the line if those prisoners escaped. However, the power of the apostles' extreme witness was such that other hardened, pagan prisoners chose to stay with them rather than make their escape. What they had seen and witnessed of Paul and Silas was such that they felt safer with them inside the prison than free and outside the prison!

The story finishes with a couple of amazing exchanges and contrasts. The jailer washes and is washed. He bathed their wounds and he was baptized. Their need was physical; his was spiritual – but they were all washed. Paul and Silas were set free from prison, and the jailer was set free in Christ. The apostles were saved from a physical jail, and the jailer was saved from the spiritual prison of sin. But they were *all* set free.

PRAY:

> *Lord, let us look with your eyes on the 'field full of harvest'. In the face of the common and ordinary, may we not be discouraged, but may we be ready to navigate in calm waters and stormy spaces, so that at every moment we may contemplate you at work in this world. In spite of all that might discourage us, may we see that true worship is in serving, obeying and adoring you, and in this way may we be faithful witnesses to you at all times. Amen.*

> CARMEN CASTILLO – REGIONAL SECRETARY, LATIN AMERICA

THE WIDER STORY

READ: ACTS 17:1–15

The first part of Chapter 17 follows the familiar pattern of the first missionary journey: Paul preaches in the synagogues, many believe, but the Jewish authorities stir up a crowd. Next, there is a riot, often accompanied by violence against Paul or those sympathetic to him, and he is encouraged to move on. Here, it is the Greek cities of Thessalonica and Berea. Note the phrase used of the apostles, that they were 'turn[ing] the world upside down' (verse 6, ESV) and also the commendation of the people in Berea that they 'searched the Scriptures day after day to see if Paul and Silas were teaching the truth' (verse 11, NLT). The words of any preacher, expositor or prophet – even those with a proven track record such as Paul had – always need to be tested against the rest of Scripture.

REFLECT:

- How do you think the apostles 'turned the world upside down' (Acts 17:6)? Where do you see that happening today through the words and actions of believers?
- Are there times when perhaps we have accepted the word of a preacher or author uncritically?
- In what ways can we develop our gift of discernment and take more time to search the Scriptures?

AN EVENING PSALM

READ: PSALM 142

It's easy to see the connection between this morning's reading and this psalm. David's spiritual and emotional prison (verse 7) is intensified in the very real prison endured by Paul and Silas who had been victims of the snares set for them by their enemies (verse 3). Like David before them, there was nowhere else they could turn (verse 4) and so they cried out to the Lord to rescue them (verses 5–6). In their desperate need (verse 6) they would know that the Lord still watched over them (verses 3, 6). Was this one of the songs that Paul and Silas sang that night? We will never know, but when they were delivered and saw one of their persecutors turn to Christ it was a fulfilment of verse 7 as they were able to use their experience to win over the jailer and his family. If you find yourself in trouble or suffering, use this as your prayer tonight. If you have experienced God's deliverance and faithfulness in the past, pray that your testimony from those days will result in others coming to know and trust him.

IN THE MARKETPLACE

READ: ACTS 17:16-34

> *While Paul was ... in Athens, he was greatly*
> *distressed to see that the city was full of idols. So*
> *he reasoned in the synagogue ... as well as in the*
> *market-place ... with those who happened to be*
> *there.*
>
> ACTS 17:16-17

One of the most stimulating times on any university campus is the week early in the first term when every club and extra-curricular activity sets out its stall and organizes events. In Europe they are called Freshers' Fairs or Society Weeks; in other places, Orientation Weeks. They usually take place in the main gathering places, the halls or courtyards in the centre of campus where all the students pass through. Every political party, every minority group, every religious or cultural society is there. And into that melting pot every year thousands of Christian students bear witness to Jesus. Paul's experience in Athens is probably the nearest we can find in Scripture to him speaking in a context like the modern university campus Freshers' Fair. It is an episode full of great variety.

A variety of locations

Paul shares the gospel in the synagogue, the marketplace and the council chambers (verses 17, 22). He spoke to the religious and the non-religious alike. Often student evangelism involves multiple contexts at once, especially if it is among international students: atheist, Islamic, Buddhist, Hindu. Even in countries with a so-called Christian tradition the contexts and assumptions will be very different between Orthodox, Roman Catholic and Lutheran believers. Some student groups even have to deal with the equivalent of the Athenian Areopagus if they have to promote or defend their activities to the university authorities who can be increasingly hostile to giving the Christian gospel 'air space'.

A *variety of audiences*

Paul speaks to Jews and God-fearers, to passers-by – an audience which, from what we know of the context, would have included a fair number of tourists out to marvel at the architecture and hear the latest interesting theories from the philosophers – and also, of course, the politicians (verses 17, 18, 21, 22). This Athenian cross section is parallel to many modern university campuses. Cosmopolitan, international, educated, but searching. The university where I studied actually had its own 'agora' where political lobby groups would 'preach' to the passers-by. There was a food stall and students would sit on the ground idly listening to whoever was speaking that day (the sugar doughnuts were particularly good). Posters and advertisements for every cause would litter the surrounding walls like Athenian idols. Sometimes the Christian Union would bring in a speaker. The response was very similar to what Paul received, but I remember occasionally taking an interested student to a quiet corner to answer their questions.

Students generally, and many internationals particularly, find that when they are away from home they are open to exploring new ideas. Often, they do not have the freedom to do this in their own country. Not all are atheists; many have given up on formal religion but retain from their upbringing (or from God's continued working in their lives!) an awareness of God. They are the God-fearers referred to here.

A variety of methods

Paul doesn't approach all these groups in the same way. His evangelistic and apologetic methodology is tailored to the audience. He doesn't come with a formulaic approach; he varies his methods. We know he was a great preacher (many times in Acts we hear of him expounding the Scriptures), and here we read of dialogue and debate (verse 17) and, in front of the Areopagus, a defence (*apologia*) of the Christian faith. This was essentially an 'apologetics address'. Paul was demonstrating that the Christian faith was true and could more than hold its own against the prevailing philosophies of the day which did not satisfy or deliver.

A variety of illustrations

Paul grounds his theology in the context into which he was speaking. He referenced their culture, their landmarks (verse 23) and quoted their poets (verse 28). He was always looking for links and bridges to the gospel, to illustrate how Christ was king over all the earth and was calling everyone to return to him (verse 30).

Even while there are all those varieties of location, audience, methods and illustrations, underneath it all, of course, there is an unchanging message. Paul's message included all the ingredients of a good evangelistic talk: he identified with his audience, sought to persuade them of the truth and invited them to respond. In his address you will see him mention creation (verse 24); God's sustaining (verse 25), sovereignty (verse 26); imminence (verses 27–28) and transcendence (verse 29); the need for human repentance in the light of the coming judgment (verses 30–31); and the proof of all this in the light of the ministry, death and resurrection of Jesus Christ (verse 31).

A variety of reactions

What was the response? What we have here is the normal reaction when you preach or hold an evangelistic event: some mock, while others listen but don't commit (verse 32). The postponing may be an excuse ('I'm just not interested') or it may be genuine ('I need more time'). But there are often those who believe (verse 34).

Paul was not amazed at the architecture; he was distressed by the lostness of the people. He saw the city and its citizens the way Jesus sees them. We will be more missionally-minded, more evangelistically-engaged, whenever we start identifying the idols in contemporary hearts that prevent our friends and neighbours from worshipping Jesus and find ways of pointing them instead towards the true and living God.

The best way to be missionally-motivated is to hold on to the assurance that only the gospel of Jesus Christ has the power to change lives for the better and give humanity a hope and a future. It is true – and it is also good.

Some say that Paul failed. But what is interesting is not necessarily the number but the legacy, the endurance and the influence of those who believed. We still remember two of their names today, thanks to Luke's account – one of them even has a main road in Athens named after him, the 'Odos Dionysiou Areopagitou', right beside the Acropolis and the site of Mars Hill. Among the many, God always has his few.

PRAY:

> *Lord God, who made the world and everything in it, you are Lord of heaven and earth, and you give everyone life and breath. You command all people everywhere to repent and have set a day when you will judge the world with justice by your risen Son. Thank you that you made all the nations so we could inhabit the whole earth, and you have appointed our times in history so that people would reach out for you and find you. As you have called us to be your witnesses around the world, please help us to proclaim the Good News of Jesus as we encounter people from many backgrounds with many different ideas. Help us to speak of Jesus and his saving work clearly and to live for him in all our lives. And may many come to believe and trust in you as Lord and Saviour. Amen.*

BEN CARSWELL – GENERAL SECRETARY, TSCF NEW ZEALAND, PACIFIC REGION

THE WIDER STORY

READ: ACTS 18:18 – 19:10

Tomorrow we will look at Paul's experience in Corinth. The second half of Chapter 18 details the period between the two riots in Corinth and in Ephesus. Paul covers a lot of miles, but ends up in Galatia and Phrygia, and, as well as doing his usual evangelistic, apologetic and expository teaching, we see another important aspect of these journeys: his ministry of strengthening and encouragement (verse 23). We then hear of Apollos, a zealous and enthusiastic preacher, but one whose theology was incomplete in some significant areas (verses 25–26). What we see here is a case study both in patient discipling (on the part of Aquila and Priscilla) and teachability (on the part of Apollos). As a result of the former's constructive mentoring, the ministry of Apollos was even more fruitful, powerful and Christ-centered (verses 27–28). There are also echoes of this in the first incident in Chapter 19, when Paul discovers a group of followers in Ephesus who are confused about some very basic gospel truths and whom he instructs and brings to a fuller understanding of faith through the Holy Spirit (19:1–7). In verses 8–10 the pattern continues as Paul again is opposed in the synagogue, so he decamps to a lecture hall where, subsequently, he has a really fruitful two-year ministry. Note how sometimes entire years of ministry are passed over in Luke's selective account, yet these are the times of steady work when many people come to faith.

REFLECT:

- Fundamental to the success of Apollos's ministry was his teachability. How do we respond when an older Christian may correct or rebuke us? Defensively? Humbly? Thoughtfully?
- Paul is not discouraged easily. When he meets a group who don't know Jesus or the Holy Spirit, he doesn't accept their religious experience as valid: he tells them the truth; when he is opposed in the synagogues, he goes to a lecture hall. When are we most tempted to give up too early or easily? Or when do we see steady years of ministry as less important than quick spectacular 'successes'?

AN EVENING PSALM

READ: PSALM 97

As Paul's heart was stirred to preach the uniqueness of Christ amidst all the idols and gods of ancient Athens, so this psalm proclaims the supremacy of *Yahweh* over all other gods. He has all the powers of nature at his disposal, because he created and sustains the earth (verses 1–5). In the light of all this power, other idols appear worthless and useless (verses 6–7). Yet, while God will judge those who oppose him, the psalmist calls for all other gods and their worshippers to turn and recognize *Yahweh* and bow down before him. The psalmist wants their salvation not their destruction (verse 7). The psalm finishes with a reminder that this comparison of the gods is not like a battle of earthly powers where defeated nations had to cope living under whichever king came out on top. No, compared to the shame the psalmist speaks of in verse 7, living under the rule of *Yahweh* brings joy and salvation, love, life and light (verses 8–12). As we saw this morning, our idols do not need to be physical images. Think of the desires or ambitions that may be *your* idols at the moment, and pray that they would be dethroned from your heart so that the living God can take his rightful place in your life; so that you would truly know the joy and light of verse 11.

TAKE COURAGE

READ: ACTS 18:1–17

One night the Lord spoke to Paul in a vision: 'Do not be afraid; keep on speaking, do not be silent. For I am with you, and no one is going to attack and harm you ...'

ACTS 18:9–10

The challenges facing Christians today are not new. Paul was completely aware of the counter-cultural nature of what he was saying. This was particularly true in the cities of Corinth (and also in Ephesus in Chapter 19). This part of Acts gives us a little insight into the courage it takes to be a disciple of Jesus.

Courage to believe in a really hard place (Acts 18:1–4)

There were two things about Corinth that made it unpromising territory for the gospel. Firstly, the culture was completely over-sexualized. Up on the hill in the centre of the city was the temple to Aphrodite, the goddess of love, and the female attendants roamed the city street as prostitutes during the night. There was a phrase in Greek: 'to act the Corinthian', which meant to be promiscuous, and Corinthian girls were called 'whores' by the rest of the empire. Paul's letters to the believers in Corinth show that it was a struggle for them to shake off the promiscuity that was part and parcel of the culture. This was a hard city in which to be a Christian.

Secondly, not just the pagans, but also the Jewish religious people, were totally opposed to the Jesus

Movement. The majority of the Jewish ruling classes despised this message (see 1 Corinthians 1:22–23). Religion can keep people away from Jesus as much as sexualized paganism. The call to repent and believe the gospel is a costly one, and it puts us in opposition to many sections of our society. It takes courage to believe in a really hard place.

Courage to believe a really great message (Acts 18:5–8)

Paul reasoned, argued, debated and discussed with them (verses 4, 19) even though they regarded his words as nonsense (like some Athenians in yesterday's reading). The gospel is not anti-intellectual; it did not conform to the limits of Greek philosophy (see 1 Corinthians 1:18), but that is not the same as saying that it doesn't make sense. It is the same today; it is seen as foolishness not to live for yourself, not to pursue your own happiness above all else. Our peers may think it is stupid for us to live as a Christian: to follow a Christian sexual ethic, to give a proportion of our time and money explicitly to God or to give up a potentially lucrative career to work with students or in a church. But none of those things are irrational; they just don't conform to conventional wisdom. When a person is converted, their mind is changed (Romans 12:2) but so are their heart and emotions (Romans 10:9). Paul *reasoned* with the Jews and with the Greeks. An important part of IFES' mission is to show that, even in academia, God reigns!

Of course, some *were* persuaded! Titius Justus (verse 7) and the ruler of the synagogue, Crispus, a man of note in the community with so much to lose, were prepared to sacrifice career and reputation for the sake of Christ. In verse 17 we read that Sosthenes, another synagogue leader, was the next one to be beaten. In the first verse of

Paul's later letter to Corinthians (1 Corinthians 1:1), we read that he was with a Sosthenes – probably the same man now writing back to his home town, a co-worker with Paul.

I am often humbled when I meet some of my colleagues around the world and hear of the sacrifices they have made to follow Christ: many have been disowned by their families, some have forfeited promising careers, some have even lost their jobs. One young academic was told that if he ever wanted to have a reputation, he needed to give up Christianity. He asked his accuser what he could offer instead of Christ. When the professor was silent, the young man said, 'Well then, I'll take my chance with Jesus'. He went on to be a renowned author and academic.

Courage to trust an amazing Jesus (Acts 18:9–11)

As we read about Paul's experiences in Corinth we see how God *provided him with friends for the journey.* In verse 2, we meet Aquila and Priscilla. Then, in verse 5, Timothy and Silas come bringing encouraging news and unexpected gifts. Right at the time when he needed it for his gospel ministry, God provided Paul with the resources (2 Corinthians 11:9; see also Philippians 4:16).

God also *provided places to go and people who would listen.* Paul and his companions are thrown out of the synagogue but a place opens up right next door (18:7)! This is the testimony of so many student groups around the world. One door closes and another opens. The university inexplicably double books the room and they have to de-camp somewhere else, which turns out to be far more appropriate. Or the university won't let them use the premises but someone lends them a room in the local café or pub, and it is the most successful night they have ever had.

A student story

Sam was a student in the United States from a Tongan family. At a missions conference he heard God's call to return and help plant a student movement in his homeland. He raised the finances and was ready to go when the Covid-19 pandemic occurred and the islands were closed to all outsiders. Not knowing what to do, he consulted with others in the United States and Pacific region, and they began to think creatively about whether there was somewhere else suitable for Sam, with his background and vision. And so Sam went and lived in Guam. There had been a desire to start a student movement there. As a US territory it was not closed to Sam, and there were also sufficient cultural similarities between Polynesia and Micronesia to make this an ideal fit. One closed door had led to an unexpected but fruitful open door for pioneering ministry.

So too here, in the home of Titius Justus, there is unexpected fruit. Paul gets the hearing his own people refused to give him, and it is here that Crispus and his family finally come through for Christ and are baptized. God gave Paul people like Crispus, Aquila and Priscilla, and Timothy and Silas to keep him going.

But above all, God *provided himself*. He spoke directly to Paul and gave him specific comfort and guidance (verses 9–10). Here it was in the form of a real vision: 'Do not be afraid … I am with you.' Paul may have been tempted to worry that Corinth was just going to be another city, another beating, another riot, another expulsion, another few days running away from the authorities. But the Lord comes himself to comfort him and says: 'I have many people in this city' (verse 10). There was a harvest in Corinth for Paul to reap. People lived there who didn't know yet that they were God's people, that he had his hand on them, but they were there, and God tells Paul to stay. Perhaps you feel like giving up in your ministry, or moving on, or just keeping quiet about your faith, and God wants to encourage you today; to remind you that he has his people in your city or your campus, and you shouldn't be afraid to reach them.

So Paul stays for eighteen months. Look at what he did during that time: he taught the Word of God (verse 11). That was his method, everywhere he went (see Acts 13:6–12). When the Bible is faithfully taught, God speaks by his Spirit. Luke, in this chapter, reports just the one vision of one night, in which the Lord told Paul to keep on speaking. Paul then persevered for a further eighteen months – over 500 more nights – without waiting for another vision; teaching from God's Word in obedience, encouraging this young church in the difficult place that was Corinth, and bringing others into the faith.

PRAY:

My Father and my God, you are so wonderful in your ever unfathomable works. I pray that when, according to your plan for my life and the ministry to which you have called me, I should find myself in a place where living my faith would be difficult – or a place where witnessing to the gospel would be difficult – you would give me the grace to persevere by standing firm rather than giving up. Open my eyes and my understanding Father, to your presence, your power and the greatness of your work in which you have sovereignly engaged me. God, make me sensitive always to your encouragement, your assistance and your fidelity

which never fail. Allow me to live with the certainty
that you always give what you command and that
your presence in me is the only 'fully comprehensive
risk guarantee' I need at all times, in all places and
in all circumstances. Thank you, Father, that my
life is precious in your sight. Amen.

KLAINGAR NGARIAL – REGIONAL SECRETARY,
FRANCOPHONE AFRICA

THE WIDER STORY

READ: ACTS 19:11 – 20:16

This period was also marked by extraordinary miracles
(verses 11–12). It is clear that these were genuine
works of God, because when some tried to mimic the
exorcisms it turned out badly (verses 13–17). In fact, this
period of ministry in Ephesus was characterized by an
explicit confrontation between the work of the apostles
inspired by the Holy Spirit and occult practices (verses
18–20). The climax of the chapter, however, is the riot
that erupted in Ephesus as a result of the downturn in
the magic and idol business through the success of the
apostles' ministry (verses 21–41). It portrays the sinister
dynamics of mob rule: motivated by self-interest;
playing on fear, rumour and misrepresentation; and
characterized by confusion and contradiction. Chapter
20:1–16 charts the next part of the travelog, including
the colleagues who supported and accompanied Paul,
and tells of the miraculous raising of a young man in
Troas called Eutychus (the patron saint of anyone who
has ever fallen asleep during a sermon!).

REFLECT:

- When the Holy Spirit is at work, the powers of darkness are confronted. When have you witnessed or experienced a particular oppression or darkness as you have tried to be faithful?
- Read Ephesians 6:10–13 and pray that the light of Christ would dispel the darkness in that situation or person.
- Look at the roll call of Paul's companions in Acts 20:3–5: ordinary disciples ministering to him at this demanding time. Who has walked with you as a 'Sopater' or an 'Aristarchus'? Give thanks for them and perhaps let them know how much you appreciated their fellowship and guidance when you most needed it.

AN EVENING PSALM

READ: PSALM 140

This is an honest psalm, and it could easily have been one of those prayed by Paul during his days in Corinth and Ephesus. Certainly, David had plenty of opportunities to express these feelings when he was on the run from Saul or when he was plotted against by members of his own family. On the surface it is a simple request that those who plot violence should be thwarted. He portrays evil coming from every part of their bodies: hearts (verse 2), mouths (verse 3), hands (verse 4), heads (verse 9), and he prays for a full protection from the Lord so that his feet (verse 4) and his head (verse 7) are shielded. He asks that their own actions would rebound on them and that those who hunt him would themselves be hunted by disaster (verses 9, 11). This is not, however, just a selfish cry for revenge. It is a heartfelt longing for God's justice to be established in the land instead of slanderers so that the poor and needy would be vindicated and that God's name would be praised and honoured (verses 11–13). It is verse 10 that we may find difficult if we are living relatively safe and prosperous lives and moving in polite company. But when these words are prayed without any hint of personal malice and purely out of a cry for justice against violence, they are entirely biblical. They are not at variance with Jesus' commands to love our enemies; they are simply realistic about what the natural end will be for those enemies if they do not repent.

Recently, a pastor from Ukraine told me that while sitting night after night in bomb shelters, those gathered turned regularly to these psalms as spiritual comfort that evil would not triumph. Use this psalm tonight to pray for a situation where you long for justice and for God's protection against your enemies.

AN EMOTIONAL GOODBYE

READ: ACTS 20:17–38

Keep watch over yourselves and all the flock of which the Holy Spirit has made you overseers.

ACTS 20:28

We have been blessed to see many students come to faith through the witness of Christian student groups across the globe. We also understand that the key to real fruitfulness in ministry is not only having a strong evangelistic emphasis, but also a rigorous commitment to discipleship and mentoring in faithful gospel obedience and spiritual disciplines. This is especially true in the days post-conversion before the new believers have got settled in a good Bible-based church community, but it is also true for all our students as we teach them how to lead well and feed themselves spiritually in preparation for taking up leadership in their churches in the years ahead. An emphasis on evangelism without an equal commitment to discipleship is a little like running a maternity ward without providing any post-natal care.

We think of Paul as an evangelist and a theologian, but here we see him as a pastor: one committed to strengthening the new believers and exhorting them to remain faithful in the difficulties they will soon face (see Acts 14:22; 15:41; 18:23). In his interaction with the Ephesian elders we notice several significant things about his discipleship practice.

It is intentional

Paul is entering the final stage of his mission as recorded by Luke. The remaining chapters focus on his legal testimonies as he appeals to Caesar (see 'The Wider Story' below). His mind is set on first going to Jerusalem. He had decided to sail past Ephesus (verse 16) but felt he could not leave the area without seeing the leaders of that church one more time. He had had a fruitful ministry of more than two years there, in spite of the riot recorded in Chapter 19. He was aware of the probable challenges lying ahead for the church, so he intentionally asks them to travel to meet him. He took seriously the health of these young churches.

It is focused on the essentials

You can tell what is important to someone by listening to them when they know their time is short. There is no time given to minor issues or disputes. Paul reminds the Ephesian elders of the primacy of proclaiming the gospel (verses 20–21) and the necessity of conversion to Christ. Whatever other ministries we may be involved in as a student group or a church, we must not forget that our central duty is to call people to repentance and faith.

It is Spirit-led

It is the Holy Spirit who has compelled him to go to Jerusalem (verse 22); it is the Holy Spirit who has warned him of the dangers ahead (verse 23); and it is the same Spirit who has appointed and will empower these elders to guard and protect the church in Ephesus (verse 28). All our strategies, all our programs, all our planning will be in vain unless we are listening to and guided by God's Holy Spirit. Often, we think of Paul as a great missionary strategist.

But if we read Acts closely we see that it is actually the Holy Spirit who is the strategist: guiding, leading, even closing doors in order to open others (see Acts 16:7). Paul encourages the Ephesian elders by reminding them that this Spirit is always to be behind their ministry.

It encourages compassion and generosity

The false dichotomy between acts of gospel proclamation and acts of justice and mercy is still blighting the church in too many places. There is the perception that you can separate the two, so we have people talking about 'gospel ministry' and 'justice ministry'; 'word ministry' and 'deed ministry'. Each group can be dismissive of the other, believing on one side that the others have a 'diluted gospel', and on the other side, that they are pushing a 'social gospel'. Paul knew nothing of this. As he focused on preaching repentance and faith, his last words to these elders exhorted them to help the weak and the poor (verse 35).

It is realistic and demands resilience

Several times Paul mentions trials and suffering (verses 19, 22–23, 29). He does not shy away from warning the Ephesians that there will be hard times ahead. Yet for both him and them, the suffering was never the dominant issue. Paul counted his life as nothing, and was simply determined to finish the race (verse 24; see also 2 Timothy 4:7). As for the Ephesian elders, they were saddened only by the fact that they would not see him again. Spirit-led disciples are also prepared for hard times. It can be tempting to associate the work of the Spirit only with revivals or certain spiritual gifts. But the work of the Spirit can be seen in the daily and long, drawn-out process of discipleship.

A student story

Ragnhard leads a student group in the small Atlantic archipelago of the Faroes. A strongly nominal Christian culture, his context is far removed from the paganism of Corinth or Ephesus. So a few years ago he began a weekly discipleship school with a handful of young students, naming it *Sendibod*, meaning 'ambassador'. Each year he had to add an extra layer to the teaching as the students wanted to stay and dig deeper. After only four years he had a full program in place culminating in several students being trained to deliver parts of the course to the first years and assisting in overseas missions.

Similarly, the work of the Spirit may be seen in places, not just of dry nominalism, but also of persecution, as Paul warned. These can be periods of humbling, winnowing and exile. Sometimes it may be our role to be a 'Jeremiah' or an 'Ezekiel' to those in exile; sometimes we might be like an 'Elijah on Carmel' or a 'Jonah in Nineveh' witnessing a revival. Our future may involve being a 'Peter at Pentecost' or a 'Paul in prison'. Philip experienced both (see Day 21). There was a work of God in the heat of revival among the hundreds, but an equal work of God in the heat of the desert with the one. Whatever God has in store for us, our role is to be ready and available.

PRAY:

> *Heavenly Father, thank you for your Word and for the example of the apostle Paul. I pray and humbly ask you for your guidance and assistance as we spread your Good News among students. Please, help us to minister, not according to our own knowledge or experience, but I pray for each one of us that we*

would allow our plans and actions to be fully directed by your Holy Spirit. Lord, as your servants, we come before you and ask you to give us the courage to persevere in sharing your message to students; to be inspired by the scriptural example of Paul; to keep our focus on the need for 'repentance'; and to teach our students the way to become strong and firm disciples of Christ. In the precious name of Jesus, I pray, Amen.

MARC PULVAR – REGIONAL SECRETARY, CARIBBEAN

THE WIDER STORY

READ: ACTS 21:1 – 25:27

From Chapter 21 onwards, Paul is resolutely set on going to Jerusalem (21:1–16) in spite of prophetic warnings that he would be arrested and possibly killed. Despite doing what he could to avoid provoking the Jewish leaders (verses 17–26), they still stir up the mob (verses 27–40). He has to be rescued by the Roman commander and is given permission to address the crowd. (For the way Luke describes the incoherence of the riots in Acts, compare Acts 21:34; 19:32.) The next chapters contain successive speeches from Paul as he makes his defence and gives his testimony. But they are not identical. The parts of his story and the aspects of the gospel which he selects are carefully chosen according to the audience. In Chapter 22, he speaks in Aramaic to the Jewish authorities, but mentions the vision he had from God to leave Jerusalem and go to the Gentiles (verses 17–21). In the ensuing riot he uses his Roman citizenship to prevent a beating. In Chapter 23 he stands before the Sanhedrin and speaks of the resurrection to cause a rift within the ranks of his accusers. Paul learns from his nephew that there is a plot to kill him and he escapes under armed guard who bring him before Felix the Governor. In Chapter 24, Paul concentrates on his post-conversion ministry and emphasizes his faithfulness to the Scriptures. Knowing of Felix and Drusilla's adulterous relationship, and of Felix's tendency for corruption, Paul also speaks of 'righteousness, self-control and … judgment' (24:25) which pretty much ends the conversation and leads to Paul being left in prison for two years. Chapter 25 sets the scene for tomorrow's conversation with Agrippa. Felix is succeeded by Festus who asks Paul if he will return to Jerusalem, but Paul appeals instead to Caesar and sets his sights on Rome. Festus doesn't quite know what to do with Paul so he consults his guest, King Agrippa, who asks to hear him speak.

REFLECT:

- Examine these chapters to consider how Paul:
    - Uses politics, including religious politics, to his advantage.
    - Does not look for conflict but is ready for it when it comes.
    - Varies his approach and emphasis according to who he is speaking to.
- Do you have God-given privileges, experiences, talents or relationships that you can use to open doors for the gospel?
- Think of a gospel conversation, speaking opportunity or testimony that you may have in the near future. What aspects of the gospel will speak most directly or be most challenging to the audience?

AN EVENING PSALM

READ: PSALM 73

I have a confession. This is possibly my favourite psalm – or at least in my top five! It begins with a statement of faith, but the first half of the psalm is an honest statement of disappointment with God because of the apparent injustices in the world (verses 2–14); the wicked live long and prosper while the good are faced with troubles. Maybe you can identify with verse 13. It is as if the psalmist is saying 'What is the point? I have tried to be faithful to God for no purpose; I would have been better off enjoying myself' (verses 13–14). The psalmist is 'thinking out loud', but as he listens to himself, he realizes he is looking at things from the wrong angle. His bitterness and blindness to the bigger picture have made him 'stupid' (verses 21–22, NASB) – it has actually dehumanized him. The turning point comes when he goes to worship with God's people (verses 16–17). In the context of worship these things have stopped troubling him, because he sees things from God's perspective.

When we are feeling disappointed or angry with God, when we lose perspective, the worst thing we can do is distance ourselves from the fellowship of other Christians. We will never get perspective by retreating into our own thoughts. Verses 23–26 are the high point of the psalm. They would have been an appropriate accompaniment to Paul's thoughts at the end of his life (compare 2 Timothy 4:18). Just as there is sadness in Paul's words as everyone has left him, yet there is the assurance that God has been faithful to him. Finish the day by making verse 28 of this psalm your meditation. Stay close and take refuge!

DAY 29

A CLEAR TESTIMONY

READ: ACTS 26:1–32

> *But God has helped me to this very day; so I stand here and testify to small and great alike.*
>
> ACTS 26:22

One of the most effective elements in student ministry and evangelism is the use of personal story or testimony. While students will want answers to questions and may listen carefully to an invited guest presenting the truths of the gospel, they are often more impressed when one of their peers stands up and recounts how this gospel message has changed their life. So telling our story is an important part of witness. Over the past few days, we have seen Paul preaching, debating, dialoguing and reasoning with his opponents. Now we hear him testifying. In fact, this is the fullest account we have of Paul's testimony. He tells us things here that Luke did not record in Acts 9, and as we look through it, we can see some elements of a good testimony.

He tells of the past only to contrast it with the present

Too many testimonies spend a disproportionate amount of time on the pre-conversion days, cataloguing all the things the speaker did, but with no real purpose. While we may think that this is 'the exciting bit' that people want to hear, such testimonies usually end up glorifying or romanticizing sin, and can leave those with a less 'colourful' background with the wrong impression that how God has worked in *their* lives is not interesting or worthy of mentioning. Paul mentions his upbringing (verse 5) but immediately switches to the present. He shows that the answers he and his friends were seeking have been fulfilled in Christ, and the hope that was being sought in years of dutiful religion has now been explicitly revealed in Jesus (verses 6–8).

He accepts responsibility but also points out the inconsistencies of his opponents

Good testimonies will acknowledge the guilt and the wrong that we did. They will not explain it away, but help our listener understand that there is such a thing as universal guilt, and we all stand in need of forgiveness. Paul does this, but also illustrates the guilt and hypocrisy of those who oppose him. There is something deeply ironic in that Paul is on trial for his life now that he has left behind his murderous ways. His previous persecution went unpunished; in fact, he points out twice that he was authorized to go on these murder sprees by the very people who are now accusing him (verses 10, 12). However, he doesn't deny responsibility (verses 9, 11) and he builds up the picture of his own guilt in preparation for telling of his conversion.

He majors on his encounter with the risen Christ

Sometimes testimonies seem to be no more than an account of a spiritual experience, an enlightenment or just a change of mind. On occasions they seem to be promoting nothing more than a new moralism, and we struggle to find out what the speaker has actually told us about Jesus. The centrepiece of Paul's testimony is his encounter with the resurrected Christ (verses 13–18).

Here, he gives us fresh insights into what he saw and heard that day. Christ asked him why he was persecuting him, and told him that it would be painful to resist any longer (verse 14), like an ox who would kick against the spiked stick that the farmer used to point it in the right direction. Jesus seems to be implying that Paul knew the right way and that all this persecution was his way of diverting his attention away from the right path. Now it was time to give up, because otherwise he was going to hurt himself and others even more.

He outlines what conversion involves

A testimony need not contain every part of the gospel message, but it will be weakened if we leave out major factors such as repentance, forgiveness, our inheritance in Christ, and our call to obedience and good deeds (verses 18–20). Paul also emphasized that this is not a cosmetic or superficial change of mind, or a choice of a new religion; it is nothing less than a transformation from 'darkness to light' and from 'the power of Satan to God' (verse 18). Conversion is radical. Good testimonies will demonstrate this in such a way that not just the cynics and atheists will hear it, but that nominally religious people will also recognize that, without an encounter with Christ and a conviction of their own guilt, they are equally guilty.

The response

We saw how, in his apologetics talk in Acts 17 (Day 26), Paul had a variety of responses. The same happens here in terms of his testimony. Festus thinks he is insane (verse 24) while Agrippa seems more thoughtful. He disguises this with a sarcastic comment (verse 28) but

Paul's honest response and integrity (verse 29) appear to have convinced him of Paul's innocence (verses 30–32). Not every testimony or talk will reach the hearts of every listener. There will likely be those who scoff or mock, either as a defence mechanism, or because their minds are darkened (see 2 Corinthians 4:4). But those who are reasonable will at least listen thoughtfully and know there is a case to be made. It is easy to dismiss an argument; it is not so easy to dismiss a person (especially in the West where personal narrative and self-identity are highly regarded). In the university mission context, often the testifier will discover that afterwards, people will want to quietly discuss with them elements of their story that they found challenging.

Learn to tell your story the way Paul told his, and pray that God will use it for his glory.

PRAY:

Oh Lord, I give you glory. You knew me when I was formed in my mother's womb. You had a purpose and design for me from the beginning. Though I have strayed, you have brought me into a secure and focused relationship with you. I desire that you would use me to share the wonders of new life with everyone I meet – and would that not stop until the Good News has reached the ends of the earth. Give me boldness and sensitivity to share my story and proclaim the Good News in a way that connects with everyone I meet. And may you receive all glory as others follow you and devote themselves to making you known among the nations! Amen.

KURT THIEL – REGIONAL SECRETARY, NORTH AMERICA

THE WIDER STORY

READ: ACTS 27:1 – 28:10

Paul's final journey towards Rome doesn't go smoothly. It is a difficult sea passage ending in shipwreck but, in no small part due to Paul's witness and integrity, there are no fatalities. Even in this story of shipwreck we see Paul respected by those in charge: allowing him freedom to make a shore excursion to see friends (verse 3); letting him take initiative (verses 21, 31–35); and ultimately commanding that his life be spared (verse 43). 'As one man, by his integrity and hope, can save the lives of almost 300 people; so the church in its feebleness as a minority can have an effect on the wider community and culture.'[5] Upon landing at Malta, Paul's miraculous protection from a snakebite at a bonfire led to him being declared first a murderer, then a god! (28:4–6).

REFLECT:

- When and where do you feel most powerless as a Christian? What encouragement can you draw from the experience of Paul in these chapters?
- In this episode Paul seems more focused on his calling by God to go to Rome than on his own rights, comfort or even freedom. How can the example of Paul and the faithfulness of his God inspire us to put our calling first, rather than our comfort, freedom or rights?

---

5 Vinoth Ramachandra, 'The Christian in the world; reflections on Acts 27', Address to Senior IFES Staff, Nairobi, June 2022.

AN EVENING PSALM

READ: PSALM 119:161–168

This section of the great Psalm 119 about God's words and laws begins with a scenario where the psalmist is persecuted by those in power (verse 161). We saw this morning how Paul was pushed from ruler to ruler and, like Jesus before Pilate and Herod, how he stood firm on God's promises, understanding that these earthly authorities did not have ultimate power. The power of God's Word to speak into every area of our life means that we can both tremble at it (verse 161) and rejoice in it (verse 162). Above all we are to *love it* (verses 163, 165, 167). This is the main point of this section. Even when it challenges us in our thinking or behaviour, do we truly love it? Do we love it enough to follow and obey it (verses 166, 168)? Yes, God knows all our ways (verse 168), but he wants that fact to be a comfort not a terror to us. It will only be a comfort when we know his character as revealed in his Word. Pray tonight that you will love God and his Word more each day, and that as a result you would know the 'great peace' that is promised in verse 165.

THE GOSPEL IS NOT CHAINED!

READ: ACTS 28:11–31

> *[Paul] proclaimed the kingdom of God and taught about the Lord Jesus Christ – with all boldness and without hindrance!*
>
> ACTS 28:31

And so, the story ends. Or does it? As we anticipate some kind of closure to the story of Paul (and we may be disappointed) we do see a few things which remain central to the character and life of the apostle.

The importance of companions on the journey

The first sixteen verses of this chapter read like a travel blog, but notice the role of other nameless 'brothers and sisters' who welcomed, walked with, encouraged, gave hospitality to and doubtless prayed with Paul on his last journey (verses 14–15, 30). In his final letter from Rome, Paul makes clear how much this fellowship means to him (2 Timothy 4:9–12, 19–21). Companions who share and speak into our lives are vital. We cannot begin the journey without them and we certainly can't finish it without them. Those, especially leaders, who cut themselves off and try to 'go it alone' inevitably make themselves vulnerable to failing spiritually and morally.

Gracious in relationships

Paul could have been excused if he had decided to spend his time waiting for his trial by focusing on his own troubles and just enjoying the comfort of the other Christians. However, his heart was still breaking for his own Jewish people. Even though the leaders of this community were responsible for his suffering, as soon as he arrives, he calls the local Jewish leaders and shares his testimony with them (verses 17–22). Soon even more of them come to listen (verse 23).

Bold in convictions

As we read verses 23–28, we see Paul continuing to do the same things that had characterized his ministry from the earliest days: witnessing, explaining, persuading, before issuing one final warning. He says that because of their unbelief, and in fulfilment of Isaiah 6:9–10, this gospel message with all of its covenant promises is now being preached to the Gentiles, who are ready to accept it (verse 28). Paul was always ready to witness to his own people, but he was equally prepared to take full advantage of new opportunities, being convinced that the Good News was indeed for all people. His graciousness in continuing, even under house arrest, to keep his door open for those who distrusted him (verse 22) did not cause him to compromise his gospel convictions or shy away from warning people of the consequences of their disbelief.

Confident in God

Paul's boldness is also emphasized in the final verse of the book. The last thing we see of Paul in Acts is that he is 'proclaim[ing] the kingdom of God … with all boldness and without hindrance' (verse 31)! We can only finish the race with this assurance if we have retained an unwavering confidence in God. Nothing any of his opponents had said in the debates and discussions had dented this confidence; he knew their empty religion had nothing better to offer. Nothing any of his opponents had done to him by way of beatings or persecutions had caused that confidence to slip; he knew his God had brought him through them all. He could remain in chains under house arrest and know with assurance that the unchained gospel would still spread and God would achieve *his* purposes regardless of Paul's personal limitations.

We are not told Paul's final fate. But in terms of God's timeless revelation to us, we have been told all that we need to know. The story of Paul finishes here, but the story of Jesus continues. The story of all that Jesus continues to do and teach (see Acts 1:1) goes on in your life and in mine. It continues in churches; in the gathering places in universities and in the campus dormitories; in bold acts of proclamation and in conversations in coffee shops; in public campaigns for justice and in secret acts of mercy; in debates and dialogues; and in group or one-to-one Bible studies. The story continues to be written as Jesus' disciples share the gospel in word and indeed throughout the world.

CS Lewis finished his *Chronicles of Narnia* by referring to 'the Great Story which no one on earth has read: which goes on forever: in which every chapter is better than the one before.'[6] This is the story of God's mission. As Paul himself wrote in his final letter: 'God's word is not chained' (2 Timothy 2:9). As Jesus promised, the gates of hell will not hold back the steady progress of his church (Matthew 16:18).

My journey of faith, like many who are reading this, has been deeply shaped by ministries such as IFES, and

6 CS Lewis, *The Last Battle* (HarperCollins, 2010), p172.

the staff and students there have been my companions on the journey. We can testify to *seventy-five years of God's faithfulness* as we have sought to hold firmly to the message entrusted to all believers. But it is only a beginning. More chapters are to be written by you and by future generations: often in hardship, sometimes in persecution, always in weakness. But we have this assurance: 'that he who began a good work in [us] will carry it on to completion until the day of Christ Jesus.' (Philippians 1:6). The gospel is not chained!

> Happy if with my final breath
> I can but gasp his name;
> Preach him in life, and sing in death
> 'Behold, Behold, the Lamb!'[7]

CHARLES WESLEY

PRAY:

Father God, we thank you for the tenacious witness of the apostle Paul, the unlikely candidate that you chose to carry the gospel message from ancient Judea to Rome, the centre of political power at that time. From there your church has continued to grow, and today you have entrusted the gospel into our hands. Lord, we cannot carry this responsibility in our own strength. Please fill us with your Holy Spirit and enable us to be your faithful witnesses among the students and communities to which you have called us, and to the ends of the earth. Amen.

TIM ADAMS – IFES GENERAL SECRETARY

7 Charles Wesley, 'Jesus! The Name High over all' 1749, hymnary.org (accessed 16 March 2023).

THE WIDER STORY

Much of the rest of the New Testament contains letters (both to churches and to individuals) written by Paul during the years of these journeys and imprisonments. Read them as the journal of a man who knew what it was to fulfil the commission of Acts 1:8.

AN EVENING PSALM

READ: PSALM 100

One of the most influential evangelical theologians of a previous generation, JI Packer, would often say 'theology is for doxology';[8] that is, we *learn* about God in order to *praise* God – doctrine should lead us to worship. During this study, we have looked at many of the core doctrines of Scripture: creation, redemption, incarnation, atonement. This morning we left Paul anticipating the return of Jesus the King, a promise that should fill us with hope, expectation and wonder, and lead us to praise. Psalm 100 is loved around the world and has been sung on many special occasions, and in the past, even at national celebrations. It is a psalm which reminds us that we are his creatures, but creatures that are loved and cared for (verse 3). It proclaims that God is good, that his love is eternal, and that he is faithful through all generations (verse 5). These are truths that are simple but profound, and which we need to be told again and again when so many others in our culture doubt his goodness, or question his very existence. As believers we need to keep preaching the gospel to ourselves and each other,

8 JI Packer, *Concise Theology: A Guide to Historic Christian Beliefs* (InterVarsity Press, 2011), pxii.

reminding ourselves of these truths often. That is why this simple psalm should be engraved on our hearts and minds. A day is coming when we shall enter the gates of heaven (see verse 4) and the eternal praise party will begin. Until then we can worship him with our imperfect but joyful songs (verse 1) praising him for his faithfulness through all generations.

There are many musical versions of Psalm 100, traditional, contemporary, and through all cultures. Use one that you know, or find one online and use it as your praise offering to God tonight.

THE IFES STORY SO FAR ...

Throughout 2023, IFES celebrated its 75th anniversary. Events were held around the world, culminating at an international gathering in Indonesia, the World Assembly, in August 2023.

The IFES story is one of the growth of an international student movement, of the hard work, persistence, prayers and generous support of countless people around the world and, above all, of the faithfulness of God.

The story began on the university campuses of the UK and the USA in the late 19th century. God inspired men and women to form national evangelical student movements which themselves birthed evangelical missionary movements that spread the gospel message around the world.

In the 1930s, 'International Conferences' brought together evangelical student ministries with a shared desire to form an international fellowship that would serve to encourage and promote gospel ministry amongst students around the world. From this, IFES was officially inaugurated in 1947 with a vision to see 'a clear witness to Jesus Christ established in *every* university in the world'.

A global fellowship with a global vision!

From 10 founding member movements in 1947, IFES has grown. By 2023 there were 164 member movements, with IFES-related ministry in a further 19 countries. Over the years, in order to support the ministry of the national movements, IFES has organized itself into 11 regions: North America, Latin America, Caribbean, Europe, Middle East and North Africa, Francophone Africa,

English- and Portuguese-speaking Africa, Eurasia, South Asia, East Asia, and South Pacific to provide support and advice for the movements. In addition, Global Resource Ministries and an International Services team based in three locations – USA, UK and Malaysia – provide practical support and ministry resources.

Our 75th anniversary has been a wonderful opportunity to celebrate the faithfulness of God and marvel at the many stories of his impact in and through students, campuses and wider society. The vision to see the gospel shared in every university in the world remains but whilst we have much to celebrate, we also understand that this is an 'unfinished story'. All that has gone before serves to build our faith, trust and confidence to move into the next season with expansive, expanding and expectant hope.

THE GROWTH OF A GLOBAL MOVEMENT:

National movements in the following countries have affiliated with IFES over the last 75 years.

- 1947 Founding conference in Boston, USA with 10 founding movements – Australia, Canada, China, France, the Netherlands, New Zealand, Norway, Switzerland, the UK and USA
- 1950 – Sweden
- 1953 – Germany, Mexico
- 1956 – Japan
- 1959 – India, Italy, Philippines, Singapore, South Korea
- 1963 – Brazil, Hong Kong, Peru, Puerto Rico
- 1967 – Argentina, Denmark, Finland, Malaysia, South Africa, Venezuela
- 1971 – Dominican Republic, Ghana, Nigeria
- 1975 – Chile, Iceland, Lebanon, Pakistan, Spain

- 1979 – Colombia, Fiji, Kenya, Papua New Guinea, Portugal, Thailand, Uganda, Zambia, Zimbabwe
- 1983 – Jamaica, Liberia, Malawi, Sierra Leone
- 1987 – Austria, Bangladesh, Bolivia, Eswatini, Guatemala, Honduras, Israel, Paraguay, Sri Lanka, Tanzania
- 1991 – Angola, Belgium, Canada (Quebec), Hungary, Nepal, Poland
- 1995 – Benin, Burkina Faso, Burundi, Cameroon, Chad, Costa Rica, Croatia, Czech Republic, Ecuador, Ethiopia, Madagascar, Mali, Niger, Panama, Serbia/Montenegro, Slovakia, Suriname, Uruguay
- 1999 – Albania, Barbados, Bulgaria, Central African Republic, Congo, Côte d' Ivoire, Democratic Republic of Congo, El Salvador, Estonia, Gambia, Guinea, Guyana, Ireland, Latvia, Lithuania, Mauritius, Nicaragua, Romania, Senegal, Togo, Trinidad & Tobago, Ukraine
- 2003 – Belize, Indonesia, Lesotho, Rwanda, St Lucia
- 2007 – Armenia, Botswana, Egypt, French Guiana, Gabon, Georgia, Guadeloupe, Haiti, Jordan, Martinique, Moldova, Mozambique, Namibia, North Macedonia
- 2011 – Antigua, Bosnia, Slovenia
- 2015 – Greece, Macao, Mongolia, Palestine, South Sudan, Syria
- 2019 – Cambodia, Cayman Islands, Faroe Islands, Grenada, Guinea-Bissau, Montenegro, Myanmar, Solomon Islands, St Vincent and the Grenadines, Vanuatu
- 2023 – Bahamas, Taiwan

In addition to these, there are member movements in an additional sixteen countries which we cannot name for reasons of security. God knows each one.